Above & Beyond

Basics

Karen Kay Buckley

American Quilter's Society

P. O. Box 3290 • Paducah, KY 42002-3290

Located in Paducah, Kentucky, the American Quilter's Society (AQS), is dedicated to promoting the accomplishments of today's quilters. Through its publications and events, AQS strives to honor today's quiltmakers and their work – and inspire future creativity and innovation in quiltmaking.

Library of Congress Cataloging-in-Publication Data

Buckley, Karen Kay.
        Above & beyond basics / Karen Kay Buckley.
            p. cm.
        Includes bibliographical references and index.
        ISBN 0-89145-866-2
            1. Patchwork–Patterns.   2. Appliqué – Patterns.
        3. Quilting–Patterns. 4. Quilts. I. Title.
        TT835.B77   1996
        746.46 ' 041–dc20   96-27192
                                                     CIP

Additional copies of this book may be ordered from: American Quilter's Society, P.O. Box 3290, Paducah, KY 42002-3290 @ $18.95. Add $2.00 for postage & handling.

Acknowledgments

I feel so very fortunate to be sharing this, my second book, with you. I could not have done so without the help of the persons listed below.

First I would like to thank the American Quilter's Society for allowing me to share my work again. A very special thanks to Meredith Schroeder and Marcie Hinton for all of their help.

Thanks so much to Helen Sheibley for being one of my best quilt buddies. We have shared some wonderful experiences together, and I know there will be many more. Thanks, Helen, for loaning me fabric when I ran out, helping with my classes, and for all of your support. But most of all, thanks for not being upset when the project you worked on for this book was eliminated. That is the sign of a true friend.

A special thanks to my other quilting buddies, Barbara Schenck, Lytle Markham, and Carmen Eiserman, who are always willing to go on another fabric trip, help come up with ideas for names of books and quilts and give me words of encouragement.

I would like to thank the following students for allowing me to use their quilts in this book. Thanks to Barbara Schenck, Michelle Howe, Kathy Cashman, Ivy Greenawalt, Diane Nesbit, Kay Lynn Orth, Kelly Bailey, Donna Hemler, and Mary Rhyner.

Thanks also to some special students for their help. They are Sally Ackroyd, Kathy Eberwein, Cheryl Runyan, Charles Kemberling, Barbara Shope, and Joan Boegel.

A very special thanks to Mary Jo Kurten for being such a big help with the editing. It was so wonderful to work with someone who knows how to edit *and* quilt!

I save the best until last. I have the most wonderful husband anyone could want. After I returned from a quilting trip, the guild president wrote and said they now have what they call the "Joe Scale". This is the way they will measure their spouses, with Joe being the top. What a great compliment for someone to receive. Several of my friends are trying to determine how to clone him! All I can say is I got lucky, and I am thankful every day for the support, encouragement and time Joe gives me. Without him I would not be sharing this book with you or presenting such beautiful quilts to be viewed. From the bottom of my heart, thank you, Joe, for the best 15 years of my life. You are the kindest and most generous person I have ever met. I am looking forward with great anticipation to sharing the rest of my life with you.

Contents

Introduction

For the past year I have been designing new quilt patterns and teaching them. The response has been great. The nice thing about teaching the classes before the book goes to print is that all the patterns have been tested. The main purpose of this book is for you to have fun learning new techniques: from hand appliqué to quick piecing and from machine appliqué to machine quilting, and be able to complete the projects quickly without sacrificing accuracy.

Quilting has become a wonderful and major part of my life. I feel very fortunate that throughout these past several years my husband has not only supported my love of quilting but has himself become involved in many of my pursuits. His encouragement and my love of quilting instill great joy in the making of each new project. Every quilt I have made has been special to me in one way or another. While piecing a new quilt for each of my brother's and sister's newborn children, I wondered what these babies would look like as children and adults, and, in years to come, how they might appreciate the work Aunt Karen had devoted to their special quilts. Since my family understands the great amount of time that goes into the making of a quilt, I know they will pass this on to their children. As I quilted a Friendship quilt, where each block was made and signed by a member of the County Line

Quilters, I remembered all the times I had spent with each person and the fun things we did together. I have made some fun and wild quilts with a special person, like my husband, in mind. Sometimes knowing the person to whom the quilt will be given helps me focus on the quilt. Thinking of the person gives me ideas, and the quilt begins to grow. When each quilt is completed, I hang it on my design board and critique it and hope others will enjoy the result as much as I enjoyed making it. I hope each of you enjoys the patterns I have designed for this book and has fun making them for yourself or for others.

I have completed over 200 quilting projects. I never realized I had done so many until I began compiling a photo-journal of my work. I was enjoying the making of each quilt so much that I lost track of the numbers. People find it hard to believe I have made so many quilts in such a short period of time. After working in an office atmosphere for many years, I've learned to manage my time wisely. I do not run errands every day, but plan to do them once a week. This does not always work out – but it sure helps when it does! I have no children, but my dog, Sammie, and my husband, Joe, sure do find plenty to keep me busy. I never sit idle. When I watch television, I do some hand sewing or look through some photographs or pictures for ideas for new quilts. A former boss asked me how I found the time to quilt, and I asked him how he found the time to play tennis. We both decided that you make the time to do the things you love. So, make the time and have fun!

My first book, *From Basics to Binding: A Complete Guide To Making Quilts* (AQS, 1992), focuses on the basics. It is oriented toward the beginner and anyone looking for additional patterns; it includes 50 12-inch block patterns and offers basic reference material.

Above and Beyond Basics begins with a glossary of products and equipment you will need for your work. Section I: Beyond Basics, gives you advice and helpful suggestions to complete the projects in Section II. You'll learn tips about selecting, preparing, and cutting fabric, as well as information about constructing, finishing, and cleaning projects. These techniques may be a review of methods you have previously tried or mastered, but I have added some of my own suggestions, and I hope you'll learn from them and have fun with the projects.

Products & Equipment

Today, quilters have an almost overwhelming variety of good tools and products from which to choose. In my list I've identified products that work for me. Try to experiment with as many kinds of equipment as you possibly can and find your own preferences.

BIAS PRESS BARS® – Used to make narrow appliqué strips and stems. Pat Andreatta of Heirloom Stitches (626 Shadowood Lane, Warren, OH 44486) markets Bias Press Bars®. They are heat resistant and come with four sizes in one package.

CHALK WHEELS – Used to mark dark fabrics. There are several different brands and all work well. There is loose chalk inside the holder and a wheel at the bottom where the chalk is released when rolled along the fabric. Place it against the edge of a ruler and roll it gently to make a fine line for quilting. Chalk brushes off during quilting, so you need not worry about permanent lines remaining on the surface of the quilt. Mark only a small area, quilt it, and then mark the next small area.

Chalk comes in colors, but some do not brush off and may remain in the fabric permanently. I recommend using only white chalk wheels. If you use colored chalk, test it first.

CORNSTARCH AND CINNAMON – Handy kitchen items that can be used to mark fabrics. Cornstarch is used to mark dark fabric, and cinnamon is used to mark light fabrics. Using gauzy fabric or cheesecloth, make a square, several layers thick. Place a few tablespoons of cornstarch or cinnamon on the layered cloth. Close the cloth around the powder and tie a knot, making a little ball.

By rubbing or lightly pounding the ball over a precut stencil, small particles of cornstarch or cinnamon are released onto the fabric. The technique is much like the chalk wheel; mark only a small section at a time. This method is wonderful for machine quilting on darker fabrics. (See the quilting design on the "Rose Trellis".)

CUTTING BOARDS AND MATS – Several brands and sizes are available. For practical use, the smallest you would want to purchase is 17" x 23". I like to work with a board with grid lines to keep my cuts straight. There are several good brands. Check availability in your area. These boards are self-healing. After the cuts are made, the board simply heals itself. Keep your board away from heat. Do not store it in the car where heat can warp it, and never place anything hot, like a cup of coffee, on top of the board.

DARNING FOOT – Used for free-motion machine quilting. May have a round, oval, or rectangular opening. Check your accessories box; not all machines come with a darning foot. Some machines have one foot for true darning and a larger one for quilting. Check with your sewing machine dealer if you're not sure about yours.

DESIGN WALL – Used to assist with the visual planning of your quilt. When you place blocks or portions of your quilt on the design wall, you can see how various elements work together. The colors, shapes, balance, movement, and overall design can be seen better on the design wall than at arm's length.

Elsewhere in this book, you will find directions for building a design wall.

EVEN-FEED OR WALKING FOOT – Used for all straight-line machine quilting and for attaching binding to quilts. This foot helps feed three layers through the machine evenly. The finished piece is more even and flat than if machine quilted using a regular foot. Most machines do not come equipped with a walking foot, so it must be ordered.

FREEZER PAPER – Used to make templates and for some appliqué techniques.

GLUE STICKS – Water-soluble glue in stick form is used for some appliqué techniques. It is safe for fabric and not permanent. The glue will dissolve when the project is washed.

INTERFACING – Medium-weight interfacing is used for one of the appliqué techniques described in this book. Do not use iron-on, fusible interfacing.

IRONING AREA – Located close to your sewing area, it will make pressing seams easier. You can use a traditional ironing board or a small pressing mat.

LIGHT BOX – Used to trace designs for appliqué or quilting onto background fabric. Other ways to transfer patterns without a light box are explained elsewhere in this book.

MARKING PENCILS – A word of caution: all markers can be heat-set into fabric. Especially with appliqué, we tend to mark an area for placement, then press the area before layering to quilt. The heat from the iron can permanently set the marked lines into the fabric. Test for this potential problem by marking a piece of your fabric, ironing over the marked lines, and washing the fabric the same way you are planning to wash the quilt. Check to make sure marked lines have been removed by washing. If marks remain on the fabric, do not use that marker!

NEEDLES – Use 80/12 needles in your machine when piecing and machine quilting. Use 70/10 or 60/8 when doing machine appliqué. Replace the needle at the end of each project or after 10 hours of use.

For machine quilting, use a sharp needle, not a ball point.

When working with metallic or rayon fabric, consider using a Metafil® or metallic needle. Metallic and rayon threads seem to break easily, but rarely with these needles.

Use Betweens or quilting needles for hand quilting in a size that is comfortable for you. Most quilters start with a size 8 and gradually work up in number to a smaller size. Remember, the smaller the needle, the smaller the eye.

Use long darning needles for hand basting a quilt. They have a sharp point, are very long, and make quick work of basting.

For hand appliqué, use what are sometimes called appliqué needles, or English Sharps, which are very fine and thin.

NEEDLE THREADER – Clover makes a very nice needle threader that has two sides. One side is for fine, the other for larger-eyed needles.

OPEN-TOE EMBROIDERY FOOT – Great for machine appliqué because it allows you to see more of the area you are stitching. Again, check with your dealer. These feet will vary in shape and price from one manufacturer to another.

ORVUS® – This cleaning agent is used to pre-wash fabric and finished quilts. It can be found in some quilt shops, tack shops, and feed stores. It is a horse shampoo. It has been the number one cleaning agent for washing quilts for the past ten years, because it does not fade the colors or cause any harm to the fabric. Many detergents cause discoloration of fabrics after only one washing.

PENCIL SHARPENER – Marking and drawing tools need to be sharpened frequently. Keep a small sharpener nearby at all times.

PERMANENT MARKERS – Used mostly for signing quilts. I prefer the Pigma® brand. They make a very fine line and do not bleed into the fabric. Remember, they are what they say – permanent. They can also be used on the quilt's surface to do special notes, poems, signatures, and drawings.

PINS – My favorites are silk pins. They are great for machine piecing and for hand and machine appliqué. These very fine, small pins do not distort the fabric. Larger pins on the seams push the fabric down so the seams and points do not line up. With silk pins, my points and seams meet almost all of the time!

PLASTIC TEMPLATE MATERIAL – Some pieces cannot be cut easily with a rotary cutter, so you will need template plastic. The advantage of plastic over paper or cardboard is that the size never changes, no matter how many times you trace around the template. This keeps your pieces accurate. Template plastic comes with or without printed grid lines. I prefer the nongrid for everything. The grid lines do not always fall where you need them and then the lines become confusing. I also prefer to use frosted plastic rather than clear plastic. Clear plastic is hard to mark accurately because it has a glare.

QUARTER-INCH MASKING TAPE – Placed next to seams, you can quilt along the edge of the tape for accurate ¼" wide quilting lines. For curved lines, use a product called Quilt-a-Flex® tape. Do not leave tape on fabric when you are not quilting. Residue from the tape may leave marks on the fabric.

RETAYNE® – This product, marketed by Pro Chemical & Dye, Inc., and others, is used to set the color in fabric. It can be used only on fabric pieces; do not to use this on a finished quilt.

If you have a piece of fabric that will not stop bleeding, try Retayne®. The instructions for use are provided with each bottle. It is not expensive, really does work, and does not fade fabric.

ROTARY CUTTER – The right cutter can make an incredible difference in your work. I have tried several brands, but still prefer Olfa®.

Some cutters have a hard and soft switch. Try each to see which is easier to use. On some cutters you can loosen a screw to allow the cutter to work more smoothly.

Cleaning and oiling your cutter will also make a difference. Carefully take the cutter apart, laying each of the pieces down in the order removed to ensure that it goes back together properly. Wipe the blade with a small piece of cloth to remove lint. Place a small dot of sewing machine oil between the blade and the safety shield. A simple cleaning will make the cutter work more smoothly.

RULERS – I prefer Omnigrid® rulers because the lines are printed very accurately and are easy to read on light and dark fabrics. Rulers should be at least ⅛" thick to allow cutting with the rotary cutter, and you should be able to see through it. Before buying a ruler, place it over several different fabrics to see how easy it is to read. If you do enough cutting, it is worth investing in the sizes you think you will use most. A larger size is handy for cutting borders.

SAFETY PINS – Used for some appliqué techniques and for machine quilting. Use nonrusting pins, just in case they are in the fabric longer than you plan for them to be. Nickel-plated size 1 safety pins have a sharp point and do not harm fabric. You may need many pins for machine quilting, depending on the size of your quilt. With pins every 3–4 inches, you will probably need 400 to 500 pins for a full-size quilt.

If you have a choice, purchase safety pins open. It takes time to open all of the pins needed to baste a quilt. As you remove them from the quilt, leave them open and return them to their container ready for use. Many dry cleaners will order safety pins for you.

SANDPAPER – Fine grain sandpaper is used by many to stabilize fabric while marking lines for sewing. Place the fabric wrong side up on the grain side of the sandpaper and mark the fabric. The sandpaper grips the fabric for more accurately traced lines. Some quilt shops sell sandpaper boards that have the paper secured on a thin board to stabilize it.

SARAL® PAPER – Used to transfer quilting lines or pattern lines onto fabric. Some quilt shops carry it, but it is more easily found in art and craft supply stores. It can be purchased in sheets or on a roll.

SCISSORS – You will need both fabric scissors and craft or paper scissors. Buy the best pair of fabric scissors you can afford. Proper tools make your projects easier and more fun. I have many pairs of scissors, but my Clover serrated edge and my Gingher plastic-handled scissors are my favorites. Keep your scissors sharpened. Good scissors have a screw at the hinge that can be removed to sharpen them.

Do not use your good fabric scissors to cut templates from plastic or paper. Use paper or craft scissors for cutting everything but fabric.

When appliquéing by hand or by machine, a small pair of embroidery scissors is perfect for cutting a sharp point in a small area.

Don't forget thread snippers! I keep mine on a ribbon around my neck. I have tried different brands, and I like Gingher the best.

SEAM RIPPER – Used to remove stitches. Keep one close to your sewing machine and hope you do not need to use it often!

SEWING MACHINE – Keep your sewing machine in good working order. Clean it at the end of each project or after 10 hours of sewing. It really makes a difference in how well the machine works and how much longer it will last. A brush is usually provided in the box of accessories. Use it to brush lint from under the feed dogs and from the bobbin area. Check your manual to see how often, and where, you need to oil your machine. Some machines may recommend more than one place.

For most of the work explained in this book, you only need to be able to sew a straight line. But to do machine appliqué, your machine must zigzag and have the capability for changing stitch width and length so you can do a very small blindstitch. You must also be able to drop the feed dogs to sew curved lines for machine quilting.

STENCIL BRUSHES OR COTTON SWABS – Used for my favorite appliqué technique – transferring spray starch onto fabric. One will work as well as the other.

SPRAY STARCH – Spray N' Starch® is the brand I prefer for my favorite appliqué technique. (This technique is explained on page 29.)

SYNTHRAPOL® – Marketed by Pro Chemical & Dye, Inc., and others, this product can be used on a quilt if the colors have migrated or bled when it was washed. It works best if the quilt remains wet, but if the quilt has dried, it is still worth a try. Instructions are on the bottle.

TEMPLAR® – Heat-resistant template plastic that comes in 8½" x 11" sheets and is used for turning under seam allowances. It can be ordered from Pat Andreatta, for address see page 14, or purchased at some quilt shops.

TERRY CLOTH TOWEL – Placed on top of your ironing surface, a terry cloth towel will cushion your completed appliquéd work when you press it. Remember always to turn the appliqué piece over and press from the back.

THIMBLES – When hand sewing (quilting, appliquéing, or piecing), a thimble protects your skin. Thimbles come in many sizes and designs. Find one that fits your finger and feels comfortable. If you have never used a thimble, try a long, leather thimble. It is soft and conforms to your finger.

Some quilters find it easier to push the needle from the side of the thimble rather than the top, and for this, the tailor's thimble is the best choice. It has deep dimples on the sides and has no top.

If you push from the top of your thimble, you need one that has deep dimples on the top and a lip around the edge. The deep dimples keep the needle in place, but should the needle slip, the lip will catch it.

If you have a hard time finding a thimble that is comfortable, or if you have arthritis, try the paddle thimble. It has deep dimples and it does not need to fit your finger. It is hand held and used much like a regular thimble.

THREAD – I use 100% cotton thread for both hand and machine piecing and I prefer Mettler silk-finish 50/3. It does not twist and knot like the polyester and polyester/cotton blends. It can be used on the top of the machine or in the bobbin when machine quilting.

For hand appliqué, I strongly recommend cotton embroidery thread. It is so fine that when you have completed your stitching the thread is barely noticeable. I prefer Mettler 60/2 embroidery thread, which comes on a spool.

In many instances you can use nylon thread. It comes in a smoked color or clear. I recommend the YLI brand. It is very thin and not noticeable when the quilting is completed. When sewing across several different colors of fabric, the clear thread takes on the color of the fabric it crosses, so the only thing you notice is that it is quilted. Use clear on light and medium fabrics, and the smoked color on darker colors.

Using metallic threads of differing colors in the top of your machine can be a lot of fun and give your machine quilting project more pizzazz. There are also some nice rayon threads available in solid and variegated colors.

For hand quilting, use 100% cotton quilting thread. The spools are labeled "quilting thread." It is heavier than sewing thread so the quilt layers will hold together better and longer.

WASHOUT MARKERS – Blue washout markers are made for dressmakers and the instructions recommend wiping the marked area with a wet cloth. For quilters, this is not good advice. Wiping the mark pushes the blue coloring into the batting, and it can come back to haunt you. If you use these markers, wash the quilt as soon as you are finished, in warm water with Orvus®, and the marks will wash out completely, causing no damage to your quilt.

Resources

PRO CHEMICAL
P.O. Box 14
Somerset, MA 02726

Synthrapol® and Retayne®

HEIRLOOM STITCHES
626 Shadowood Lane
Warren, OH 44486

Templar® and Bias Press Bars®

DISCOUNT VACUUM AND SEWING
45 Gateway Drive
Mechanicsburg, PA 17055

Sewing machine feet and accessories

CALICO CORNERS
341 Barnstable Road
Carlisle, PA 17013

Most supplies listed in this book

SECTION I

BEYOND BASICS

FABRIC

Selecting fabric can be the most fun of any project. Always allow yourself plenty of time. You do not want to rush and then be unhappy with your choice. Most shops have personnel who are very good at assisting you with your selections. It is always fun to have a quilt friend with you for a second opinion. But remember to go with your instincts, even if your friend or the shop personnel do not agree with you. If you love it, it will be great. Remember, it is your quilt and you are the only one who has to like it.

Work with good quality 100% cotton fabric. If you hold it to the light and it looks gauzy, do not buy the fabric. You are going to put a lot of time into the making of each quilt, so the better the quality of the fabric, the longer the quilt will be around for people to enjoy. I prefer my fabric be torn when it is purchased, not cut. Tearing the fabric reveals the true grain of the fabric, and I find there is less waste when I am rotary cutting. If the fabric has been cut, I tear the end to ensure I am working on the grain. As a result, several inches can sometimes be lost. If the shop will not tear the fabric, purchase extra. You might like to try other types of fabric in certain projects.

Grain Lines and Cutting

Fabric has three grain lines. Lengthwise grain runs parallel to the selvage. Crosswise grain runs perpendicular to the selvage. Bias grain runs at a 45° angle to the lengthwise and crosswise grains. The bias has a lot of stretch. There are times when it's advantageous to cut on the bias, but there are also times when we must avoid bias cuts. A major concern when cutting fabric is to ensure outside edges of pieces are square by cutting on the straight grains. This helps prevent rippling.

Prewashing

I prewash all of my fabrics before use and strongly encourage this practice. Clipping the corners of your fabric before washing it will prevent the edges from fraying. This technique is especially helpful on small pieces, but good to do on each and every piece of fabric.

Wash your fabric with Orvus®. (See the Products & Equipment section, page 10.) Use one to two tablespoons of Orvus® per washer load of fabric. Separate the colors as you would normal laundry; lights, mediums, and darks. Always wash deep, dark colors separately. They may bleed, and you do not want the color from the deep, dark fabric migrating into the light and medium fabrics. Very few fabrics bleed, but you need to know what to do if this does occur. Check your washer during the rinse cycle to make sure the color is not bleeding, or do the following:

Wash a piece of muslin with the darker load. Check it to see if any color migrated. For a quick check, place a small, wet scrap of the darkest fabric on top of any light print it will be near when the project is complete. Allow the fabric to dry, and then check to see if any of the darker color has transferred onto the lighter fabric. If so, Retayne®, a chemical product marketed by Pro Chemical and others, will stop color from bleeding. It is used by fabric dyers to set color, can be used in the washing machine, and does not fade color. *Retayne® should never be used on a finished quilt, but only on individual pieces of fabric.*

ROTARY CUTTING

The benefits of rotary cutting are speed and accuracy. The use of the ruler, cutting board, and cutter allows you to cut the necessary pieces for your quilt in far less time than the old method of using a template to make each cut. Because the fabric is placed on a cutting board in folded layers, you can accurately cut several pieces at one time. Because the fabric is not lifted, the cut shapes are very accurate.

If the shop where you purchased your fabric did not tear it, tear the fabric before you start. This will ensure that you are working on grain and help keep your strips straight.

How you fold the fabric will depend on how the cut strips are to be used. If you are cutting borders, fold the fabric raw edge to raw edge, keeping the selvage toward the top and bottom. Keep folding until the fabric is four layers thick.

If you are cutting strips for squares, triangles, rectangles, or trapezoids, fold the fabric selvage to selvage and then bring the fold to the selvage for four layers.

Do not layer more than four thicknesses. More than four layers makes it difficult to make an accurate cut. For anything other than borders, work from the torn edge of the fabric. Fold the fabric so the torn edges are even and do not worry about the selvage edge. Your cut strips will be straight and on grain, or very close to it. Uneven selvage does not seem to affect the finished strips. If it is really off, refold the fabric as you cut the strips.

For some projects long strips must be sewn together. For these projects fold the fabric only once so you are cutting through only two layers of fabric. This will ensure perfectly straight lines.

Place the fold of the fabric on one of the lines of the grid board. If you are right-handed, place the ruler to the left, so it is approximately ⅛" to ½" over the torn edge of the fabric. If you are left-handed, place the fabric to your left and the ruler to your right. Cut a straight edge. Do not trust the folded selvage edge to be perfectly straight. You need to cut a straight edge

and then measure from the cut straight edge. Start the cutter on the board, along the side of the ruler, and push or pull the cutter, keeping the blade tight against the ruler. Hold the cutter at an angle, not perfectly straight, with your index finger on the top edge of the cutter. Cut past the edge of the fabric and onto the board.

Always stand when you are cutting. If you sit, you cannot put the proper pressure on the cutter, and the chances of cutting yourself are greater. If you have never used a cutter, try both pushing the cutter away from you and pulling it toward you. You will get a more accurate cut when you pull the cutter toward yourself. Most of my students report that it is also more comfortable. Keep your body far enough away from the table to avoid an accident. Experiment with both methods, but remember to be very careful. This tool is very sharp.

Once your ruler is in place and you begin cutting, move your hand up or down the ruler as you go. I cut toward myself starting at the top of the ruler with the cutter across from my thumb. Keeping the cutter in place, I move my hand down the ruler as many times as necessary until I have reached the bottom of the ruler. If you find it easier to cut away from your body, start at the bottom of the ruler and work your way up, moving your hand up the ruler as you cut.

It is best to make one clean cut. Running the blade back and forth can lead to inaccurate cuts. The blade is very sharp, and the safety shield must be closed whenever the cutter is not in your hand to protect you and anyone else who walks into your sewing area.

When first attempting to master the use of the cutter, you may be faced with the following problems:

▶ The cutter is not cutting through all layers of the fabric. Try more pressure in your stroke and also check your blade. It may be getting dull.

▶ Skipped areas on the cutting line. Check your blade. There is a good chance it has a nick.

▶ Deep grooves are appearing in the cutting board. Check your blade. It is probably dull and needs to be replaced. To solve all of the above problems, replace the blade. Rotary cutting is safer, more accurate, and less work when the blade is sharp and free of nicks.

▶ The ruler keeps moving or slipping, causing inaccurate cuts. Glue two pieces of skid-free material under the ruler. Where can you find such a product? Check under your area rugs. If you have a skid-free pad, cut a small section from it. You'll never miss it. Some shops sell small pieces of this padding for use under the foot pedal of sewing machines and under sergers to keep them stationary. This product is also available in department stores for use in kitchen drawers and cabinets. Apply with water-soluble glue. For longer rulers, place a small piece of the skid-free material at both the top and bottom.

After you have practiced a few cuts using scraps, you are ready to put this new technique to real use: constructing a block. Any given block may contain squares, rectangles, or triangles of differing sizes and numbers.

Cutting Squares

To cut squares for a block, you need to know the finished size for the individual squares. For example, if the finished size of a square is 2", then you need to cut the squares 2½" to include a ¼" seam allowance on all sides. Cut a strip of fabric 2½". Then cut the

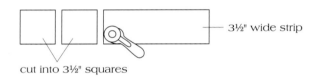

cut into 3½" squares

Fig. 1. Seam allowances are added before cutting.

Cut into 5½" sections   2½" wide strip

Fig. 2a. Calculate the best measurement for cutting.

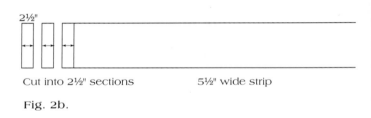

Cut into 2½" sections   5½" wide strip

Fig. 2b.

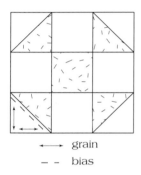

← → grain
– – bias

Fig. 3a.

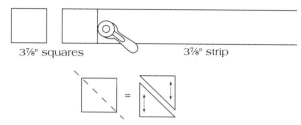

3⅞" squares   3⅞" strip

Each square cut on diagonal yields 2 triangles

Fig. 3b. How to cut half-square triangles.

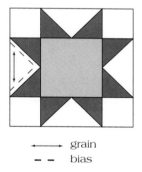

grain
bias

Fig. 4a.

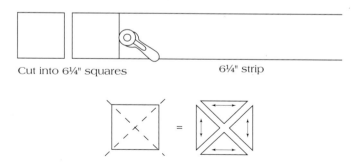

Cut into 6¼" squares   6¼" strip

Fig. 4b. A square cut on both diagonals yields four quarter-square triangles.

strip into 2½" squares. If the finished size is 3", then you need to cut a strip 3½", then cut the strip into 3½" squares (Fig. 1).

Cutting rectangles is much the same. Add ½" seam allowance to the finished size and cut strips this width. Example: If you need 2" x 5" finished rectangles you could cut your strips 2½" or 5½". It depends on how many rectangles you need. If you need 6 rectangles, cut the strip 2½", and then cut the 5½" sections from that strip (Fig. 2a). If you need 16 or more rectangles, cut the strip 5½" and then cut 2½" sections from the strip (Fig. 2b).

Cutting Triangles

Cutting triangles is very easy, but you need to place the grain properly. The outside edges of the block should always be on grain. This keeps the block square and flat. If the bias were on the outside edges, it could cause the square to stretch out of shape and ripple.

If the straight of grain needs to be on the outside edge of the block (Fig. 3a), cut half-square triangles.

First determine the finished length of the shortest side of the triangle and then add ⅞". For example, if the shortest side of your triangle is 3", you would cut a strip 3⅞". Cut this strip into 3⅞" squares, then cut each square on the diagonal yielding two triangles (Fig. 3b). Regardless of the size of the triangle side, you will always add ⅞". This will never change.

There are times, however, that you will want the bias of the fabric on the short sides of the triangle (Fig. 4a).

In that situation, which places the grain on the long side of the triangle, cut the square 1¼" larger than the finished long side. The square will then be cut on both diagonals. These are called quarter-square triangles. For example, if the long side is to be 5", the square should be cut 6¼". Cut the square on both diagonals, yielding four triangles (Fig. 4b, page 19).

Cutting Bias Strips

To cut bias strips for stems, basket handles, or stained glass, you need to know how wide and how long to make the strip. The patterns in this book include the length and width needed for each individual pattern.

Once the measurements are known, place the 45° angle of the ruler on the edge of the fabric and cut. Move the ruler over to the required width and make the second cut. If you need only one or two strips, work with a single thickness of fabric. However, if you need many strips, you can keep the fabric folded in half and cut two strips at once. Next you will need to cut along the fold. You can reduce your cutting time in half by keeping the fabric layered.

Cutting Diamonds

For 45° diamonds, as for the "Hunter's Star" project or a Lone Star or Eight-Pointed Star quilt, you can easily and quickly cut them with your rotary cutter. Add a ½" seam allowance to the finished side of the diamond. For example, for 3" finished diamonds, cut the strip of fabric 3½". Then place the ruler with the 45° angle on the cut edge of the strip and cut. Move the ruler over 3½" and repeat the 45° cut across the entire strip (Fig. 5).

Knowing how to make these cuts will save you valuable time and allow you to complete many more quilts.

DESIGN WALL

There are many benefits to a design wall. You can make one permanent, portable, or temporary, and for very little money.

The purpose of the design wall is to allow you to view blocks and pieces from a distance. You can make a temporary design wall by placing a sheet or piece of batting over the back of a door or on a curtain rod. Make sure the sheet is white, off-white, or gray, so you do not have a color interfering with your design. You can pin or tape the batting or sheet in place. When you have decided on block or piece placement, you can remove the sheet.

To make a portable design wall, purchase Styrofoam® insulation panels and tape them together to the desired size. Cover them with batting or flannel. You can pin into it, and blocks will actually stick to the batting or flannel. This board is lightweight and can be stored easily.

If you have a large wall space, you can make something more permanent. Purchase large sheets of insulation board from your local hardware store – as many as needed to cover your wall space. These panels have grooves, so they slide into each other. Cover the seams with duct tape. Use a utility knife to cut to size, then cover with white flannel.

PRESSING

"Pressing" means to apply heat and pressure to fabric without sliding the iron across the fabric. "Ironing" means to move the iron back and forth across fabric with a sliding motion.

Fabric

When I first started to quilt, I didn't realize the importance of pressing. Some quilters believe finger creasing is enough, but I strongly disagree. It does not give a crisp finished look nor does it press seams flat enough, which can later cause problems with accuracy.

Removing new fabric from the dryer when it is slightly damp makes it easier to iron. If it is

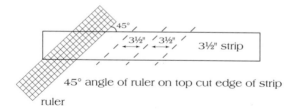

Fig. 5. Cutting diamonds.

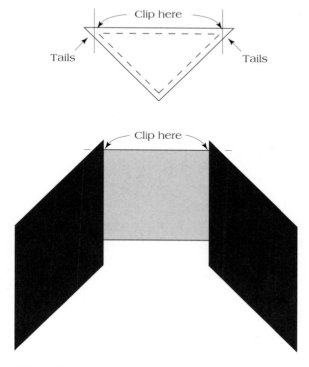

Fig. 6. Pressing seams.

completely dry, use the steam setting on your iron. If you are still having trouble removing the creases, use a spray bottle to spray some water directly onto the fabric.

Seams

Whether you piece by hand or machine, each seam should be pressed before it is sewn to another piece or section. Press all seams with a dry iron on its cotton setting. (Steaming may stretch the seams.) Press the seams from the back first, to one side or the other. Do not press the seams open. Then turn the piece over and press the seams a second time from the front.

After pressing, you'll see that triangles and diamond shapes have a tail that extends past the raw edge of the fabric. Clip these tails along the raw edge of the shape. This removes some excess fabric and makes it easier to match while sewing these pieces to others (Fig. 6).

HAND PIECING

Hand piecing takes more time than machine piecing, but if you travel or spend time waiting for your children coming and going to activities, or just like to take sewing with you, hand piecing is the way to go. Hand piecing is also very relaxing.

Hand piecing is done with a running stitch using a size 8 quilting needle and 100% cotton sewing thread. Each piece has to be marked on the reverse side of the fabric using a template as a pattern.

For a 2" finished square, you would make a 2" plastic template. Place the template on the wrong side of the fabric and trace around it. Use a piece of sandpaper under the fabric to prevent it from slipping. (See Products & Equipment, page 11.) Remove the template and use your ruler to add ¼" on all sides to create your cutting lines.

If you are sewing two squares together, place the right sides together, pin the corner points, and then pin the lines. Insert a pin on the line, then check the other side to be sure it is on that line, too. Adjust if necessary. Place a pin every inch. Sew on the line, knotting where you start and where you finish (Fig. 7).

Setting in pieces by hand is sometimes easier than doing it on the machine. Place the shape being sewn to the angle, right sides together, on one side of the angle. Pin the seam and sew from the outside ¼" to the inside ¼", making a knot at the inside angle. Do not cut your thread. Pin the second seam and sew out to the outside seam. Place a knot at the ¼", cut your thread and you are finished with the set-in (Figs. 8a, b, & c).

MACHINE PIECING

There are several differences between hand and machine piecing. Each has its benefits, depending on your point of view. Both are very accurate. Machine piecing can save you a lot of time.

Sew with a size 80/12 needle, which works well with cotton fabric. Set your machine to sew approximately 12 stitches per inch. If your machine does not have the number or stitches per inch marked, check your sewing machine manual, or do a test on a scrap piece of fabric and measure it with your ruler and count the stitches.

Use a neutral thread color for as much sewing as possible. If you are working on a project that has a variety of colors, gray thread works well. At 12 stitches per inch, you should not be able to see the thread. When sewing a three-color quilt that includes white and white touches every color, use white thread. If you

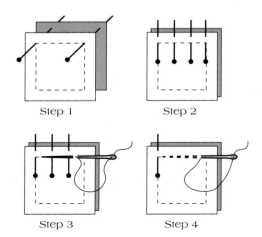

Step 1   Step 2

Step 3   Step 4

Fig. 7.

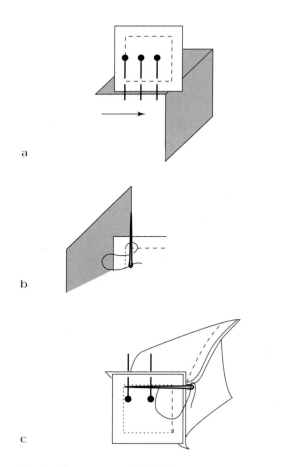

a

b

c

Fig. 8a, b, & c. Hand piecing.

are sewing and can use gray on most of the seams, but there are a few brightly colored pieces and you are afraid the thread will show, change the thread color as needed.

Seam Allowance

Cut your pieces to include a ¼" seam allowance. For example, if you need to make a template for a pattern piece, make it with the seam allowance. You will sew an accurate ¼" seam, so there is no reason to mark the lines.

Sew from the raw edge to the raw edge, in most cases. There is no reason to backstitch at the beginning or the end of a full straight seam. There are a few instances when it is necessary to start and stop sewing ¼" from the edges, like mitering a corner and setting in a shape; in these cases, it is necessary to backstitch.

Check to be sure you are sewing an accurate ¼" seam allowance. Place a ruler under the presser foot of your machine. Drop the foot gently on top of the ruler and lower the needle until it just barely touches the ¼" line on the ruler. It is rare that the edge of the ruler, which is your ¼" sewing line, will be directly beside the foot, so you will need to mark it in some manner. Having some kind of an edge or lip to sew along can make sewing easier and more accurate.

Most sewing machine manufacturers now make a quilter's foot, which is an accurate ¼" wide from the needle to the edge, so you do not need to mark the line. Some manufacturers also make a sewing guide, which screws into the machine. It can be placed along the edge of the ruler and screwed in place.

A magnetic guide can be used in this same manner, but it is not recommended for some computerized sewing machines. Check with your sewing machine dealer.

Whichever measuring device you choose

to be sure you are sewing an accurate ¼" seam allowance, feed a few scraps of fabric through the machine and check them before sewing your actual project.

Sewing Advice

Before you start sewing, pull the bobbin thread to the surface. Hold the top thread and take the needle down and up once. Pull the top thread and the bobbin thread will come to the surface (Fig. 9, page 24).

When you are ready to feed the first two pieces of fabric under the foot, hold the top and bobbin threads until you have two stitches in the fabric. This prevents the bobbin thread from knotting on the bottom.

Never pull the fabric from behind when sewing. This will cause puckering and ripples. Simply allow the fabric to be fed by the feed dogs through the machine. If the fabric is not going through easily, consult your sewing machine dealer for possible reasons.

Chain pieces as often as possible and you will save an incredible amount of time. Place right sides together; do not use pins. When you are close to the end of the first seam, place the next two pieces against the raw edge of the first set of pieces and keep sewing. Do not lift the presser foot or cut the threads. Do not backstitch at the beginning or the end. Continue until you have chain pieced all the units. Then clip the threads between the pieces and press the seams (Fig. 10, page 24).

When sewing two sections together, sew with the seam side facing you whenever possible. If you are sewing a seamless border, sew with the pieced portion of the quilt top toward you and the border underneath. There are times when both sides have seams. Choose the side that has the most seams facing you. It will be easier to control the points and the direction of the seams.

To get a good point, sew with the "X" facing you. Place a pin in the center point, at the center of the "X." This is a positioning pin. Place a pin on each side of the positioning pin, place right sides together, and secure these two pins in the fabric. Remove the positioning pin and sew right across the "X." This will give you a good point every time (Fig. 11).

Setting-In

Setting-in is necessary when you are sewing an angled seam. Sewing a set-in on the machine is only slightly more difficult than doing it by hand. Unlike most machine sewing, you need to begin and end sewing ¼" from the edges – very accurately to prevent puckers and to make sure the piece will lay flat.

HAND APPLIQUÉ

Hand appliqué, like hand piecing, is portable and very relaxing. There are times when hand appliqué will fit your schedule better than machine appliqué. In this section, several methods of turning under the seam allowance will be explained.

Use an appliqué needle or a Sharp (I like English brand Sharps). Because they are fine, they go though the fabric easily.

After several years of appliquéing with regular cotton sewing thread, I began using 100% cotton embroidery thread from a spool (not the skein) for hand appliqué. It is very fine and barely visible, and works beautifully. I now recommend it to all of my students, and their response is just like mine. "This thread is amazing." "The difference in my stitch is incredible." "Whoever would have thought the thread could make me like hand appliqué?" Try it, and you'll see!

Always match the thread color to the

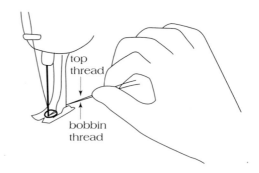

Fig. 9. Pull the bobbin thread to the surface.

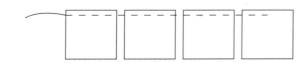

Fig. 10. Chain piece all the units.

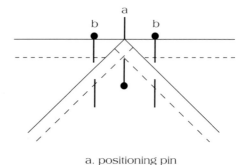

a. positioning pin
b. securing pins

Fig. 11.

appliqué shape, not the background.

When you are ready to appliqué, glue or pin the shape to the background fabric.

The Appliqué Stitch

Hold your work so the shape is toward you and the folded edge to be stitched is away from you (Fig. 12).

Knot a single strand of thread about 18" long and bring the needle and thread up through the background and about one to two threads in from the fold of the appliqué shape. The knot will be on the wrong side of the background.

Now, from the top, take the needle into the background fabric, beside the stitch you have just taken, and come back up one or two threads in from the fold. If you are right handed, stitch to your left. If you are left handed, stitch to your right. Work your way around the piece, keeping the stitches even. Twelve stitches to the inch is excellent.

Points

On an outward point, stitch up to the point. Tack-stitch right beside the point. Lift the opposite side and clip the seam allowance from under the section you have sewn. This helps to turn the point under, because some of the excess has been removed. Now, with your needle, push the seam allowance under and take one stitch straight out from the point (Fig. 13). This helps to pull the point straight and make it look sharper. Continue stitching.

Cleavage

In cleavage areas, keep your stitches closer than you would elsewhere. These are weak areas because they are so close to the raw edge. For a nice inward point, clip into the cleavage until you are one to two stitches from the actual cleavage. Push the seam allowance

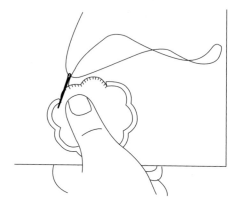

Fig. 12. Appliqué stitch.

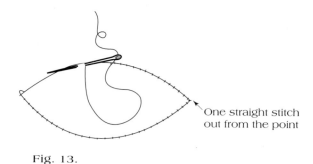

One straight stitch out from the point

Fig. 13.

under with your needle. Come in from the opposite side of the area you are stitching and pull the needle toward you; it is much easier to control (Fig. 14a and b).

Take two to three tack stitches into the cleavage, keeping the stitches close and side-by-side. (When using embroidery thread take three stitches, but if you use regular sewing thread, take only two stitches.) Stitch about three to four threads in from the fold. Then, keep making close stitches until you stitch out of the cleavage area. Remember, it is important to work with a color of thread that matches your appliqué fabric, because the thread comes in on top of the appliqué a little more than normal at the cleavage. If the thread does not match well, the thread will be very obvious.

Turning the Seam Allowance

In this section, I will explain several different ways of turning under the seam allowance of your appliqué. Many of these methods also apply to machine appliqué.

For these illustrations, a heart shape will be used because it has both a point and cleavage.

FINGER CREASING

▸ Make a template for the shape you need. Do not add a seam allowance.

▸ Trace the template onto the right side of the fabric.

▸ Cut out the shape, adding between ⅛" to ¼" seam allowance. Clip into the cleavage. Cut straight in until you are one to two threads from the traced line.

▸ Finger crease, using your thumb and index finger, on the traced lines. Fold the seam allowance toward the back of the fabric.

▸ Place the shape in position and you are ready to stitch.

GLUE STICK

▸ Make a template for the shape you need. Do not add a seam allowance.

▸ Trace the shape onto either side of the fabric.

▸ Cut out the shape, adding between ⅛" to ¼" seam allowance. Clip into the cleavage.

▸ On the wrong side, in the seam allowance area, apply some glue.

▸ Fold the seam allowance toward the back of the shape. The glue will hold it in place (Fig. 15).

▸ Place the shape in position and you are ready to appliqué.

FREEZER PAPER UP

▸ Trace the shape onto the paper side of the freezer paper.

▸ Cut out the shape on the traced lines. Do not add a seam allowance.

▸ With the waxy side down, place the freezer paper on the wrong side of the fabric. Press with a hot, dry iron. The wax adheres the paper to the fabric, holding the shape in place (Fig. 16a).

▸ Cut out the shape, adding a ¼" seam allowance.

▸ Using a dry, hot iron push the seam allowance up and over the back of the freezer paper (Fig. 16b). This will produce a very good crease, making it the exact shape of the freezer paper cutout. Clip into the cleavage.

▸ Remove the freezer paper and appliqué the piece in place.

FREEZER PAPER DOWN

▸ Make a template on paper side from freezer paper. Do not add a seam allowance.

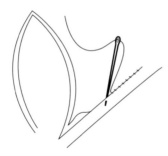

Fig. 14a. Stitch to cleavage.

Fig. 14b. Sweep needle from under leaf stem and pull down to cleavage.

Fig. 15. Apply glue to seam. Push seam back and glue will hold in place.

waxy side down

Fig. 16a.   Fig. 16b.

HELPFUL SUGGESTIONS

▶ Try each appliqué technique more than once to see which works best for you. You will find that one way works better on some shapes and fabrics than others. On one project you might use more than one technique.

▶ Pretest and use a marker that will wash out of the fabric.

▶ The seam allowance for appliqué does not need to be perfectly accurate. As long as it is close, it will work. The more appliqué you do, the less seam allowance you will want. I began with a full ¼" seam and now use an ⅛" seam allowance.

▶ When using glue to hold a seam allowance in place, glue about four inches at a time. The glue dries quickly. Be sure it is water soluble and safe for fabric. Use small amounts.

▶ When using freezer paper, remember that the waxy side sticks to the fabric. The paper side is easier to write on and to trace templates. When pressing seam allowances around a shape, press a small section at a time, especially on the curves. Use a dry, hot iron.

▶ Prewash interfacing before use because it will shrink. Some recommend wetting the interfacing, laying it flat to dry, then ironing. *Caution: do not use iron-on interfacing!*

▶ For shapes that require clipping (like the cleavage on a heart), clip where you start, and then clip as you sew around the piece. Do some experimenting. You will find there are some areas where you need no clipping.

▶ Cut the same shape from your fabric, adding a ¼" seam allowance.

▶ Center the freezer paper template over the wrong side of the fabric shape, with the wax side of the freezer paper up (Fig. 17a). Using a dry, hot iron, press the seam allowance over the paper shape. (Fig. 17b). The wax from the freezer paper will hold the seam allowance in place. Press a small section at a time. Clip into the cleavage.

▶ Do not remove the freezer paper yet. Pin the shape in place and begin your appliqué stitch (Fig. 17c).

▶ There are two ways to remove the freezer paper. You can stitch completely around the shape and then cut into the background fabric behind the shape and pull the paper out. (Cut a "plus" into the back, or cut ¼" away from your sewing lines.) The other way to remove the paper is to stitch part of the way around the shape, loosen the seam allowance from the freezer paper, and then pull the freezer paper template out from the side. After the paper is removed, finish stitching the fold on the shape. If you have stitched through part of the freezer paper, don't worry. The paper still pulls out very easily.

INTERFACING

▶ Place a piece of medium weight interfacing on the right side of the fabric you are planning to use for the shape. Use pins to hold the interfacing and the fabric together.

▶ Trace the shape, either on the back of the interfacing or the wrong side of the fabric.

▶ Cut out the shape, adding ¼" seam allowance.

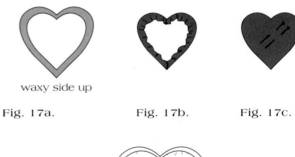

waxy side up

Fig. 17a.   Fig. 17b.   Fig. 17c.

Fig. 18a. Place interfacing on right side of fabric heart and machine stitch on traced line.

Fig. 18b. Clip straight into seam through fabric and interfacing.

Fig. 18c. Cut a "plus" through the interfacing and turn piece inside out.

Fig. 19.

▶ Machine stitch on the traced lines (Fig. 18a).

▶ This is one of the few techniques where it is necessary to clip the seams all the way around the shape. Clip straight into the seams, not at an angle (Fig. 18b).

▶ Cut a "plus" into the interfacing, at least ¼" from the sewing line, and turn the piece inside out (Fig. 18c).

▶ Use a point turner or a pencil to smooth the seam allowance.

▶ Press the shape from the front so you can be sure none of the interfacing is showing.

▶ Appliqué the shape in place.

NEEDLE TURN

▶ Make a plastic template of the appliqué shape. Do not add a seam allowance.

▶ Trace the shape onto the right side of the fabric.

▶ Cut out the shape, adding ⅛" to ¼" seam allowance.

▶ Place the shape on top of the background fabric. Using your needle, simply push the seam allowance behind the shape, using the lines marked on the top as a guide. Turn small sections at a time. As you turn the seam allowance, use your thumb to help hold it down.

▶ Appliqué stitch each section on the fold as you push it under (Fig. 19).

SPRAY STARCH

▶ Make a template of the appliqué shape using Templar®, a heat-resistant plastic. Do not add a seam allowance.

▶ Trace the shape onto the wrong side of the fabric.

▶ Cut out the shape, adding a little less than ¼" seam allowance.

▶ Place the template on the wrong side, and in the center, of the fabric shape.

▶ Clip as needed.

▶ Wet the seam allowance with spray starch, using a small stencil brush or a cotton swab. (Do not spray directly on the fabric.)

▶ With a dry, hot iron, push the seam allowance up and over the template. It will not harm your iron. Some irons get very hot and warp the Templar®. If this happens, turn your iron to a lower setting. Keep the iron on the seam allowance until the spray starch is dry. If you do not allow the spray starch to dry, this technique does not work well. Again, press a small section at a time, especially on the curves. One of the tricks to making this technique work well is to keep the iron close to the fold. Do not bring the iron in too far on the back of the shape. If there is any area you are not happy with, wet it again and re-press.

▶ After you have turned all of the edges, remove the template and you are ready to appliqué the piece in place.

BASTING

▶ Make a template. Do not add a seam allowance.

▶ Trace the shape onto the right side of the fabric.

▶ Cut out the shape, adding ¼" seam allowance.

▶ Finger press the seam allowance toward the back of the shape and baste the seam allowance in place, clipping as necessary. The basting stitch is simply a long running stitch. Use a contrasting color of thread. It is easy to see to remove later.

▶ After all of the seam allowances are

turned under, appliqué the piece in place and remove the basting stitch.

MAKING A PERFECT CIRCLE

Make a circle template from poster board or Templar® in the desired size. The template should not include a seam allowance. Cut a circle from your fabric ¼" larger than the template. Sew a running stitch ⅛" in from the raw edge. Start with a knot in your thread and stitch until you have returned to the knot. Place the template on the wrong side of the fabric circle and pull the stitch tight. The seam allowance will pull up and over the circle template (Fig. 20). Moisten the edge with some spray starch and press to dry. Remove the template and you are ready to appliqué the circle in place.

Depending on the size of the circle you need, and how many, consider using coins or metal washers for smaller circles. The metal will hold the heat from the iron a little longer, so give it some cooling time before removing the coin.

MACHINE APPLIQUÉ

Machine appliqué can save you time and most people will never know you did it on the machine. All you need is nylon thread, an open embroidery foot, silk pins, 70/10 needles, and practice. Several methods of turning under the seam allowance are explained in the Hand Appliqué section. The freezer paper, interfacing, basting, and spray starch methods can also be used for machine appliqué.

Start by turning under the seam allowance on each piece. You do not need to turn under a seam that will be covered by another appliqué piece.

Each piece should be lettered or numbered in the order of placement so the

Fig. 20. Gather the seams over the circle template.

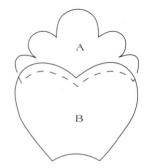

Fig. 21. Raw edge of A (bottom) is under folded edge (top) of B.

Fig. 22. A blind stitch: three straight stitches and one zig zag.

Fig. 23. Blind stitch on appliqué piece.

appliqué pieces overlap in the correct order. (Fig. 21). Transfer the appliqué design onto your background fabric. (See page 32.)

Position the pieces in order. Secure the first piece, A, in place, using several silk pins or glue to hold it in position while you are stitching. Continue to place and stitch succeeding pieces.

Use nylon thread on the top of your machine and in the bobbin.

Using the blindstitch, stitch all of the edges where the seam allowance is turned under. Baste sections that do not have seams turned under and will be covered by another appliqué piece so they do not shift during the remaining appliqué process.

Not all sewing machine manuals refer to this stitch as the blindstitch, so please read this next section, in case your manual refers to it by another name. The stitch should have between 3 to 7 straight stitches, and then one zigzag or straight stitch to the left (Fig. 22).

These straight stitches go into the background fabric along the edge of the appliqué piece. The width should be approximately ⅛". The stitch width should be wide enough so the zigzag or straight stitch comes over about two threads onto the folded edge of the appliqué (Fig. 23).

You will probably need to adjust the stitch length to approximately 20 stitches to the inch. (This is a very close stitch, so you do not want to have to rip these stitches!)

Practice on a small sample piece before beginning. If the thread looks good on your sample, go on to your project.

If your needle position is adjustable, move it to the far right. Place the open-toe embroidery foot on your machine. The folded edge of the fabric will run along the inside edge of the foot and work as a guide to help keep your stitches even.

Do not backstitch when starting and stopping. The stitch is so tight, it will not come out. If you are sewing around the entire piece, like a circle, overlap the stitches slightly where they come together. If the piece has an edge that will not be turned under, start and stop at the raw edge and the stitch will be secured by the overlap of the next piece (Fig. 24, page 32).

It is better not to start on a point if all of the edges of the shape are being turned under; start on a side. If it is a piece to be overlapped, start at the raw edge and work your way around to the other raw edge.

BIAS STRIPS

Using Bias Press Bars® makes quick work of these strips. For each bias strip needed in this book, I will give you the size of the bias strip required and how wide to cut the fabric strip. Most of the strips are cut on the bias. If they are to be cut on grain, the instructions will indicate this. Bias strips have more stretch than strips cut on the grain. If the strip has to curve, it must be cut on the bias.

To cut bias strips, place your fabric single thickness on a cutting mat. With the 45° angle of the ruler on the raw edge of the fabric, rotary cut. Move the ruler over to the recommended width. Keep the 45° angle of the ruler on the edge of the fabric at all times (Fig. 25, page 32).

Iron the Bias Press Bar® before working with it to remove the curve. (This may sound strange, but it works. If you store your Bias Press Bars® in the bag in which they were sold, you will need to do this each time they are removed from the bag.) Fold and press the strip of fabric in half lengthwise, wrong sides together. Place the bias press bar tight along the fold on the inside of the strip.

Place the zipper foot on your sewing machine and move the needle position if necessary. You will be sewing the bar inside the bias strip temporarily. Place the foot on top of the bar and sew down the right side of the strip. (Pat Andreatta recommends placing the strip with the press bar to the left and sewing along the edge of the Bias Press Bar®. I cannot keep it tight enough that way. Try both ways and see which one works best for you.) If you have a Bernina® sewing machine, a top-stitching, sometimes called an edge-stitching, foot works better than the zipper foot. If you have a Pfaff®, try the #3 foot.

If the bias strip is longer than the Bias Press Bar®, while keeping the needle down, lift the foot, and slide the bias press bar toward you as you stitch up the fabric.

Trim the seam allowance to about 1⁄16". At the ironing board, turn the seam toward the back of the bias strip. Moisten it with spray starch and dry with the iron. Slide the bar down the strip as needed. Remove the bar and the strip is ready to be sewn in place.

TRANSFERRING PATTERNS TO FABRIC

Test your markers to see which ones show best on your project's fabric. Remember to use only markers that are not permanent.

Transferring appliqué patterns and quilting designs to fabric can be done by using a light box, light table, glass door or window, window template or Saral® paper.

Light Box

If you have access to a light box or light table, this is the easiest way to transfer your pattern. Some companies now make great little light boxes just for quilters. Check your quilt shop or quilt magazine ads. Office supply stores are also a good source.

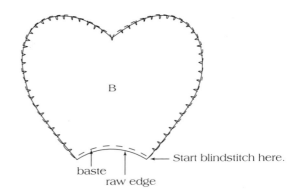

Fig. 24. Baste to hold shape from shifting while appliquéing under next piece.

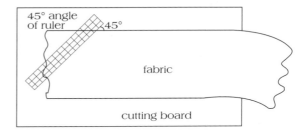

Fig. 25.

Fig. 26. Light area is plastic template material; dark area is fabric. Heart shapes have been cut from the plastic to make a window template.

Tape the pattern on the glass surface. Use repositionable tape so it does not damage your original. Center the background fabric over the pattern and tape it in place. Turn on the light and you are ready to trace, using a washable marker.

If you have a table that holds a leaf, you can make a temporary light table. Pull the table apart and place a piece of glass or plastic or a storm window in the opening. (Tape or cover any sharp edges on the glass!) Place a lamp, with the shade removed, under the opening and the light will come through producing a fine temporary light table.

If you have a window or door with a large, uninterrupted area of glass, you can use it as a light table. Tape the pattern on the glass on a bright day. Tape the background fabric over the pattern and trace.

Saral® Paper

You can also use Saral® paper to transfer designs. Tape the background fabric securely on a flat surface. Place the Saral® paper, with the chalky side down, on top of the fabric. Center the pattern on top of the Saral® paper and, with a pen or pencil, trace over the pattern. Trace a little section and then peek under to check your progress. A problem with this method is that the chalk brushes off easily, so handle the piece carefully. Since the Saral® paper comes in five colors, this is a great way to transfer designs onto light or dark fabrics.

Window Templates

Another method is to use a window template to trace the placement for appliqué pieces and some quilting patterns. A window template is made by cutting an opening in the template material. For example, in the "Crazy Lacy Hearts" project, a window template would

be very helpful to transfer placement lines for the hearts on the border. Trace the lines for the border and the hearts onto a piece of template plastic. Cut the hearts out of the plastic. Place the window template over the pieced border area and trace the heart shapes (Fig. 26).

Quilting Lines

To mark using precut stencils for quilting, you can trace the lines onto your fabric with a washout marker, silver pencil, white pencil, or by using cinnamon or cornstarch. It will depend on the fabric. If the fabric marks easily, use a washout marker, silver pencil, or white pencil. If it is a difficult area to mark, make a ball of cornstarch for the darker fabrics and a ball of cinnamon for the lighter fabrics. The powder is released onto the fabric by lightly pounding the ball over the stencil. Unfortunately you can mark only a small area at a time because it brushes off so easily.

Use a chalk wheel to mark straight lines. Simply roll the wheel along the side of the ruler. The chalk is released in a very nice, fine line. Again, it brushes off easily, so you can only mark small sections at a time.

BATTING

There are so many battings on the market. How do you know which one to choose? All battings have pros and cons. Experiment and try different ones to see which you like the best. The following covers information I have learned about each batting, by use and by contacting the batting companies.

Polyester

Polyester batting is made from plastic fibers that are blown into a web and baked. These batts come in varying thicknesses, and thickness certainly is a factor when choosing batting. The thicker the batting, the fewer stitches per inch you will be able to make. In order to avoid breaking and shifting during use and cleaning, all polyester batting manufacturers recommend this batting be quilted in 3" intervals. In other words, no more than a 3" square area should be left unquilted. This recommendation is based on the quilt receiving heavy use, so if the quilt is always going to be used as a wallhanging, you could leave a little more space open.

A common objection to polyester batting is that it "beards," which means fibers from the batting work their way onto the surface of the quilt. On quilts with darker fabric colors this is a problem. Once bearding starts, there is no way to stop it.

Because of the plastic fibers, polyester batting may lose its puffiness and flatten in later years, or after heavy use.

An advantage to polyester batting is that it does not shrink and therefore requires no prewashing prior to use.

I recommend you purchase polyester batting from a bag rather than a roll, because rolled batting is usually very stiff. The stiffness makes it more difficult to quilt.

The thinnest of the polyester battings are Mountain Mist Quilt Light®, Fairfield Low Loft®, and Glory Bee I by Morning Glory®. Because they are so thin, they are some of the easiest to quilt through and will give you the smallest stitches. These are great battings for beginning quilters!

The medium thickness polyester battings will give a puffier look, but the size of your quilting stitch will generally be a little larger than if you use thinner batting. Hobbs makes a very nice medium weight batting, as do Mountain Mist® and Fairfield Processing Corporation. Only Hobbs Bonded Fibers manufactures

black batting (really a dark gray). If you are planning to use darker fabrics and are concerned with bearding, black batting may be the answer.

Needlepunch batting is made from loose polyester fibers that have been compressed and lightly bonded. Hobbs manufactures Thermore®, Fairfield markets Traditional® and Mountain Mist® calls its needlepunch batting: Fleece. Sometimes needlepunch batting is referred to as craft batting. It is highly recommended for clothing and craft projects because it holds its shape better than any of the other polyester battings.

The very thick polyester battings are referred to as high loft or "fatt" batts. These were never intended to be quilted, but instead are recommended for tied comforters.

Cotton

Most cotton batting is made from 100% natural cotton fibers; there are a few companies that combine polyester and cotton. Cotton batting gives a wonderful antique look, which is especially appealing to some people, and it does not beard. All cotton battings are nicer to machine quilt than polyester because the cotton batting grips the fabric and holds it in place. A disadvantage for hand quilters is that cotton batting draws moisture, so it is very difficult to quilt when the weather is humid. The needle sticks in the batting and you almost need pliers to pull it out. Machine quilters will not notice any difference.

The intervals necessary to quilt vary tremendously from one brand of cotton batting to another. Some shrink and need to be prewashed. Others do not. Some people who do not prewash their fabric prefer not to prewash their batting, even though the batting shrinks. They believe the batting and the fabric will both shrink and give the finished quilt an antique look. I prewash my fabric and follow the companies' recommendations on prewashing.

Prewashing Batting

If a manufacturer recommends prewashing, follow these directions (many companies who recommend prewashing do not include any instructions): Fill your washing machine with warm water. When the agitation cycle starts, turn it off and place the batting in the water. With your hands, fully immerse the batting. Allow it to soak for five minutes. Turn your machine to the spin cycle, and drain and spin the excess water from the batting. Place the batting in the dryer, on the air cycle, until the batting has dried.

Fairfield Cotton Classic® batting is a combination of 20% polyester and 80% cotton. It is harder to hand quilt, but nice to machine quilt. Fairfield recommends prewashing the batting to remove the sizing and handle shrinkage. They also recommend quilting at 2" intervals.

Mountain Mist® 100% cotton needs to be quilted at ¼" to ½" intervals. It does shrink and should be prewashed. It is harder to hand quilt, but is easy to machine quilt. You just need to decide if you want to quilt that closely.

Mountain Mist Blue Ribbon® 100% cotton (my personal favorite) does not need to be prewashed, and needs to be quilted at 2" intervals. It is nice to hand and machine quilt.

Mountain Mist® Cotton Choice 100% cotton may come either on a roll or in a bag. The company's care instructions are provided with each cut piece. It may be quilted up to 8" apart and does not need to be prewashed.

Morning Glory Old Fashioned® 100% cotton does not need to be prewashed and can be quilted at 4" intervals. It is hard to hand quilt but nice to machine quilt. It is a very heavy batting,

so on a larger quilt the weight may be difficult to handle under the machine. However, the thickness and weight do add to the warmth.

Hobbs Bonded Fibers recommends prewashing Hobbs Heirloom® Cotton Batting (cotton and polyester blend) if you prewash your fabric. There are excellent washing instructions in each package. The recommended intervals of quilting are no less than every three inches. This batting works nicely for machine quilting.

One hundred percent cotton flannel is excellent to use as a batting or as a backing without batting. It is great for a nice, lightweight throw, table runner, or baby quilt. Since it is a woven fabric you can leave large areas unquilted and no shifting will occur. It shrinks, so prewashing is highly recommended.

Wool

Be cautious about the type of wool batting you purchase. The best wool comes from Merino sheep. Some wool battings must be placed between two layers of cheesecloth to prevent bearding. This can be a major inconvenience. Wool is a natural fiber, so it breathes. Wool has what is called "3-D crimp" that creates very small pockets that trap air, thus creating warmth and giving the batting bounce and loft. The batting will flatten after use, but as soon as the quilt is washed, the wool "recovers" and the puffiness returns. (Recovery means spring-back after crushing and creasing. Recovery is essential for maintaining warmth and shape. The recovery of wool is 95% versus 73% for polyester.) Wool batting is much more expensive than polyester and cotton.

Although there may be other comparable brands, I think Heartfelt® 100% wool is the best. Care instructions are enclosed in each bag.

Wash the batting in warm, not hot, water. The water temperature must remain constant throughout the washing and rinsing cycles. It is recommended to quilt at 12" intervals. It is a little more expensive than other wool battings.

According to Hobbs, its 100% wool batting may vary from bag to bag. Although great care is taken to coat the wool with a bonding agent, in rare cases this bonding agent may not be applied appropriately and the batting may beard. Also, the batting may beard through some poor quality fabrics. Care instructions are provided in each bag, and it is recommended to quilt at no more than 3" intervals. Hobbs is less expensive than other wool battings.

Silk

Silk batting is made before the silk strands are spun and woven. It is recommended that the batting be enclosed in silk fabric to prevent bunching and migrating. It must be hand washed in warm water. Silk batting is generally sold by the pound, rather than area size. It is used in silk quilts and silk garments, and is very expensive.

BASTING

Basting holds the three layers of your project (top, batting, and backing) together during the quilting process. It is very important to take the time to baste your quilt well.

Lay and pull the backing fabric tight on a flat surface and secure it. You can tape the backing on a table or floor, depending on the size of your piece, or you can pin it into a carpeted area. (This works best on a low pile carpet. If the carpet is too thick, the backing will not lay flat enough.)

How you plan to approach the quilting will determine how you baste your quilt. Will you hand or machine quilt? What kind of frame will you use? Do you plan to do quilt-as-you-go or quilt in the traditional manner?

If you plan to hand quilt, it is best to use thread for your basting. If you plan to machine quilt, it is best to use safety pins. Because machine quilting involves greater speed and movement, the basting threads tend to go unnoticed and may catch in the quilting stitches, making them very hard to remove. However, safety pins are easy to see, and you remove them as you get to them.

▶ To thread-baste use a long darning needle and contrasting thread. A darning needle is very large and allows you to make long running stitches quickly and easily. Contrasting thread is easy to see to remove it as you quilt.

▶ To safety-pin baste, use nickel-plated, size one pins. These do not rust, so if they are left in the fabric for a period of time you do not need to worry. (This is most unusual though, because machine quilting goes so quickly.)

▶ For quilt-as-you-go by hand, baste an X across the block and then baste around the outside edge of the block.

▶ For machine quilt-as-you-go, safety-pin baste, with the pins no more than four inches apart. This is a great way to get started on machine quilting, because the pieces are small and easy to handle. It allows you to become comfortable with the process before tackling a large project.

▶ For quilting on a hoop or hoop-on-a-stand type frame, hand baste at least every four inches.

If working on a larger frame, like a scroll frame, you can baste up to six inches apart, because the quilt does not get moved as often. Some of the newer scroll frames now

Batting Chart

Brand Name	Quilting Distance	Fiber	Content Comments
Mountain Mist Quilt® Light® Fairfield Low-Loft Morning Glory-Glory Bee	3"	polyester	Thin, will give antique look, easy to hand and machine quilt, some bearding problems, no shrinkage
Mountain Mist Regular® Hobbs Poly-Down®	3"	polyester	Medium thickness, bearding problems, no shrinkage
Hobbs Poly-Down Dark®	3"	polyester	Medium thickness, dark color batting is good for darker colored fabrics, bearding problems, no shrinkage
Mountain Mist® Fatt Batt Fairfield High-Loft®	3" – 4"	polyester	Not recommended for quilting but for tied comforter, very thick look, possible bearding, no shrinkage
Fairfield Traditional®	3"	polyester	Needlepunched, more dense, possible bearding, no shrinkage
Hobbs Thermore	3" – 4"	polyester	Needlepunched, more dense, does not beard, no shrinkage
Fairfield Cotton Classic®	2"	80% cotton 20% polyester	Some shrinkage, possible bearding, reccomend prewashing to soften for hand quilting, nice thin look
Mountain Mist® 100% Cotton	¼" – ½"	cotton	Shrinkage, easy to machine quilt, antique look, no bearding
Mountain Mist® Blue Ribbon Cotton	2"	cotton	No shrinkage, easy to machine quilt, nice for hand quilting, no bearding, antique look
Mountain Mist® Cotton Choice	8"	cotton	No shrinkage, antique look, recommended for machine needle quilting, needle-punched, bleached
Morning Glory Old Fashioned	4"	cotton	Needlepunched, easy to machine quilt, heavy, antique look, residue from leaves & stems
Morning Glory Clearly Bleached	4"	cotton	Needlepunched, bleached, easy to machine quilt, antique look
Hobbs Heirloom Premium Cotton	3"	80% cotton 20% polyester	Shrinkage, possible bearding, easy to machine quilt, antique look
100% cotton flannel	no limit	cotton	A lot of shrinkage, will lose dimension most battings give, thin, easy to hand & machine quilt, lightweight summer throw, be sure to buy good quality
Fairfield Soft Touch	2"	cotton	Bleached, no shrinkage, antique look, nice for hand & machine quilting
Warm & Natural®	10"	cotton	Residue from seeds & stems, may leave oil spots on fabric, prewash
Heartfelt® 100% Wool Batting	3"	wool	Possible bearding, more expensive, wonderful to hand quilt, easy to machine quilt, easy care instructions enclosed
Hobbs Heirloom Premium Wool	3"	wool	Possible bearding, resinated to provide stability and retard fiber migration

have a third dowel that holds the quilt top and another dowel that holds the batting and backing, and this means no basting at all. Consider this feature if you are buying a frame.

The larger, older-style floor frames also require minimal basting. The backing is basted to the fabric portion of the frame and pulled tight. The batting and quilt top are centered over the taut backing. One row of basting is sewn around the edges of the three layers to ensure the batting and top do not shift.

Remember, basting is necessary on everything but the three-dowel scroll frames, but how you baste depends on how you plan to quilt your project,

HAND QUILTING

There are pros and cons to both hand quilting and machine quilting. You may want to try each method and see which works best for you.

For hand quilting you will need quilting thread, a quilting needle, and a thimble.

Thread color is entirely up to you. When you first start quilting, I suggest you work with thread that matches the project. It will blend with the fabrics, and the size of the stitches will be less noticeable. Generally, a quilt is quilted with only one color of thread, but you can do anything you like. When you are comfortable with the size of your quilting stitch, you might want to use some contrasting threads.

▶ Start with an 18" piece of thread. If the thread is too long, it will knot and drive you crazy. Tie one end in a single knot.

▶ Use a quilting needle of a size most comfortable to you. Most quilters start with a size eight and gradually work to a smaller size. The larger the number, the smaller the needle.

▶ Position the needle so the eye is in a dim-

ple of the thimble. Holding the needle with your thumb and index finger, direct the point through all three layers.

▶ In one quick movement, push the point of the needle out onto the surface of the quilt top, placing your thumb in front of the point. You now have one stitch!

▶ Keeping your thumb in front of the point, rock the needle back and forth until you have two to three stitches on your needle (Fig. 27). Pull the needle through the layers. Some people have trouble pulling the needle out of the layers, and there are some things to help make this easier. Collins markets a product called Needle Grabbers. They are small rubber circles used to grasp the point of the needle to pull it through the layers easily. Some other hints are to wear the end of a balloon, finger cot, or rubber glove finger on your index finger.

MACHINE QUILTING

What a fast and wonderful way to get quilts finished! You need a sewing machine, darning foot, even-feed or walking foot, 80/12 needles, safety pins, and thread. (Refer to Thread and Safety Pins, pages 11 and 12.)

First, find a comfortable chair. An adjustable secretary's chair is great. The bed of your machine should be level with the table on which you are working. If it is higher than the table, the weight of the quilt is not well distributed, making machine quilting very difficult. (There are many companies who produce tables in which to set your machine. Check with your sewing machine distributor.)

You should sit squarely in front of the needle, and you should be able to rest your elbows in front of the machine, comfortably. An extension or small table to your left side is

Fig. 27. Rock the needle back and forth to take more stitches.

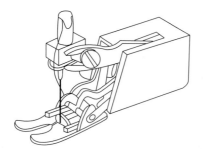

Fig. 28. For straight lines use the even feed foot on your machine.

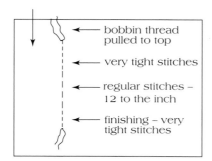

Fig. 29. Adjusting the stitch length.

helpful for holding some of the weight of the quilt while you are quilting.

If you are going to quilt a large project, roll it. Place bicycle clips around the rolls to hold them in place while you are quilting.

Straight Lines

Place the even-feed foot on your machine. Make sure the arm is over the screw on the side (Fig. 28).

Thread your machine. Fill a bobbin with 100% cotton, 50/3 ply thread. If your bobbin case has a finger, take the thread through it. Place the quilt under the needle, in the area where you want to start quilting. Take the needle down and up once while holding onto the top thread. Pull on the top thread to bring the bobbin thread to the surface. Hold onto the threads until you have two to three stitches in the quilt. This will prevent the bobbin thread from knotting on the backing. Check the tension. Thread from the top should not show on the back, nor should bobbin thread show on the surface. Before starting, do a practice piece, with the same batting you will be using in your quilt, to check the tension.

Set your machine to sew at zero, or sew in place for two to three stitches. Slowly turn the stitch length knob on your machine until you are sewing 12 stitches per inch. Stitch in place to start and then continue at 12 stitches per inch, within one inch. When you are ready to stop take the length back down to zero. Stitch in place for two to three stitches (Fig. 29).

On a straight line that is not continuous, bring the needle up and slide the quilt to the next area you want to quilt without clipping the thread. (Do not slide more than two inches!) Quilt the next area. Later, go back and clip the threads, front and back. This is called dragging the thread (Fig. 30, page 40).

Curved Lines

For free-motion quilting and curved lines, drop the feed dogs and place the darning foot on your machine. Some machines have a switch to make the feed dogs stop moving, and others have a plate to cover them. Check your manual.

Start the same as with straight lines, pulling the bobbin thread to the surface. Since the feed dogs are dropped, you are in control of the size of your stitches. It does not matter where the stitch length is set. Sew two to three stitches in place and then sew 12 stitches to the inch. End each curve by sewing two to three stitches in place.

It is good to practice control before doing the real thing. First practice meandering, and do not cross over the lines. Then meander and make loops (Fig. 31).

Quilt some straight lines. Try a zigzag or ladder effect (Fig. 32). Try making circles (Fig. 33).

Write your name (Fig. 34). You can do this by writing on the fabric or just stitch by eye.

Next, you are ready to trace a stencil design onto your fabric and quilt it. The more continuous the stencil design, the better. You want to start and stop as little as possible.

Again, practice, practice, practice. When you feel comfortable, move on to your quilt. Do not wait too long. You will be ready before you know it!

BORDERS

Sometimes when our project is complete and ready for borders, the measured sides may not be identical. But by taking the following measurements and following my instructions, you should end with straight and even borders. Measure the top, bottom, and sides of your quilt. If the project is rectangular, take the average of the top and bottom, and the aver-

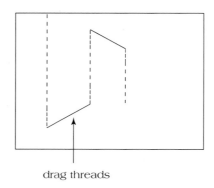

drag threads

Fig. 30.

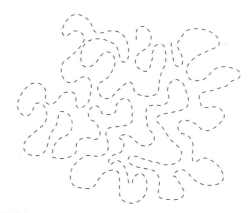

Fig. 31.

Fig. 32.

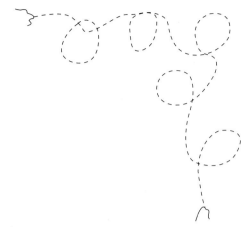

Fig. 33.

Fig. 34.

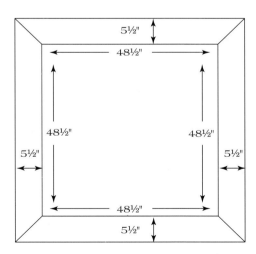

48½" + 5½" + 5½" = 59½"
Borders must be cut at least 59½" long.
I would cut these borders about 63" long
to be sure to make the miter. It is always
better to have a little extra than be short.

Fig. 35.

age of the sides. If the project is a square, average all four sides.

If you plan only one border, determine how wide you'd like it to be. Take the average measurement of either side and add to that two times the width of the border. This will tell you how long to cut the border strips for the sides (Fig. 35).

Using these figures, calculate the amount of fabric you need for your border. For example, if your finished quilt will be 78" x 50" and you want 10" borders, purchase a piece of fabric the length of the longest side. In this case, 78" or 2¼ yards. Remember always to add a few extra inches for shrinkage and mitering the corners.

If you are adding more than one border, sew the borders to each other and attach them to the quilt top as one. This way you will be mitering all of the borders at once and not doing each one separately. It is easier, and it looks better. Mitering the corners is very easy and makes the quilt look great when finished.

When cutting strips for the border of your quilt, fold the fabric raw edge to raw edge. Bring the fold over to the raw edges. Keep the fabric folded in fourths for more accurate cutting. Using your ruler and rotary cutter, cut a straight edge along the selvage to remove it. Cut four strips as long as the longest measurement and to the necessary width. You know that two of these will be longer than necessary, but it is best to cut all four strips for the border while the fabric is neatly folded.

Find the centers of the border strips by folding them in half, end to end, and finger creasing the centers. Measuring from the center, place a mark one-half the actual length of the border. Do this in both directions, from the center. Mark all four border strips.

Place one border strip right sides together with the quilt top and pin the center fold to the center of the quilt top. Place a pin through the slash marks on the border strip to ¼" from the corner of the quilt top. Sew ¼" from the raw edge of the top to ¼" at the other end of the top. Backstitch when you start and stop to make a good miter.

Sew only one corner at a time. Place the two border strips on top of each other, right sides together. Using a ruler with a 45° angle, draw a line from the ¼" stitch line on your quilt top to the outside edge of the border. The 45° angle needs to be on the raw edge of your border strip (Fig. 36).

Sewing from the ¼" on the border, sew on the line you just drew to the raw edge of the border.

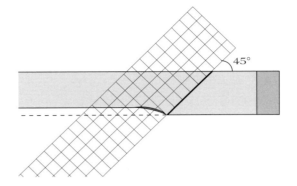

Fig. 36.

BINDING

It is always a good feeling when you reach this point. How the project will be used determines which type of binding is best. Bias binding wears better and longer than on-the-grain binding. If you plan to use the quilt on a bed or as a lap throw, use bias binding. If the project will always hang on a wall, use either type binding.

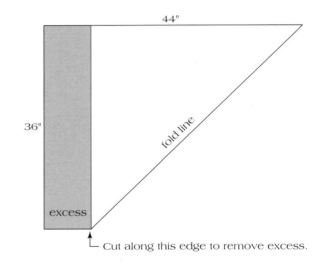

Fig. 37.

Cutting

To make on-the-grain binding, cut strips 2" wide. Sew them together until they equal the perimeter of your project.

For continuous bias binding, select the desired quilt size to determine the yardage needed.

Twin – ¾ yd.	Queen – 1⅛ yds.
Double – 1 yd.	King – 1¼ yds.

From the yardage for the size of your project, cut a square. Cut the largest square possible from your fabric. For example, if you are making a double-size quilt, the size of your

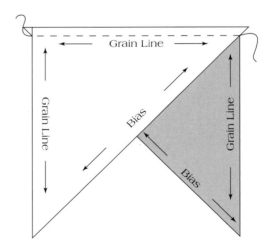

Fig. 38.

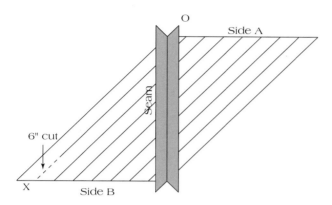

Fig. 39.

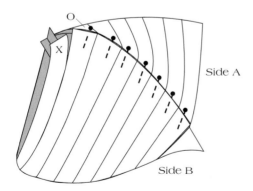

Fig. 40.

piece of fabric is 36" x 44". So, the largest square you can cut is a 36" square. Fold the corner of the fabric until it reaches the opposite side of the fabric. You will see where the square is being formed. Cut away the excess fabric. While the square is still folded, carefully cut on the fold line. You now have two large triangles (Fig. 37).

Place the triangles right sides together, so the bias is on the diagonal and the grain is on the outside edge (Fig. 38). Sew the two triangles together with a ¼" seam allowance. Do not press this seam.

Open the piece, and you will now have a parallelogram. With your ruler, draw lines lengthwise every 2" on the back of the parallelogram. Cut about 6" into the first line you drew and mark it "X." Mark the top corner of the joined triangles "O" (Fig. 39).

Fold "X" to "O" to form a seam between Side A and Side B. You need to take "X" around the back, so when you sew the seam between "A" and "B," you will be sewing right sides together. The 2" lines should meet on the seam. Pin these lines and sew the seam to make a tube. Cut where you started, on the first 2" line, to make one long, continuous piece of bias binding (Fig. 40).

After you have cut the strips for the binding you can make double-folded binding by using a bias tape maker, or make French binding.

French binding simply means binding folded in half lengthwise, wrong sides together. The raw edges of the binding will be aligned with the raw edge of the quilt.

Binding made with a bias maker looks like purchased binding. The strips are drawn through a device that double folds them. The folded strips are pressed as they are pulled out.

Attaching

For French binding, place the raw edges along the raw edge of the quilt and sew with a ¼" seam allowance.

For binding made with the binding maker, open one side and place the raw edge along the edge of the quilt. Sew in the fold that is created.

Never start sewing on a corner. It will be too difficult to make a nice miter on a corner.

This is a good time to use your walking-foot or even-feed foot attachment to your sewing machine. This attachment really helps feed all of these layers through evenly.

Sew until you are ¼" from the corner. Backstitch and remove the binding from the machine (Fig. 41).

Fold the binding up and then down, at a right angle (Fig. 42).

Place the piece back in the machine and start on the raw edge of the corner. Backstitch and keep sewing until you reach the next corner (Fig. 43).

Close the miters that are formed in the corners with hand stitches.

SIGNING YOUR QUILTS

The question is not if you should sign your quilt, but how and where. You can sign your quilt on the top along the border seam or in one of the blocks.

If you place only your name on the surface of the quilt, make a label for the back of the quilt to include: your first, maiden, and married names; the year or years the quilt was made; and the city and state where it was made.

Either write on the backing fabric or make a label and appliqué it on the back. You can keep it simple, or do something more intricate.

First, stabilize the label by ironing a piece of freezer paper to the back of the fabric you

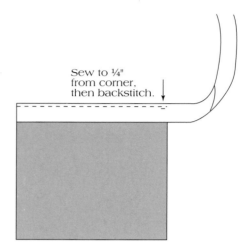

Sew to ¼" from corner, then backstitch.

Fig. 41.

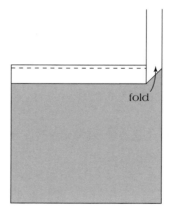

fold

Fig. 42.

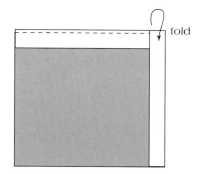

Fig. 43.

Fig. 44.

are planning to use. This keeps the marker from skipping.

Or, you can embroider the information, but first make sure your thread is colorfast by testing it. Sewing and craft stores usually have a list of the thread numbers that may bleed or migrate. If the store does not have the list, cut a small section of thread from the skein, wet the thread, and place it on a piece of wet muslin. Wait until the thread and fabric are dry and see if the color has migrated. If it has not, it is safe to use. If there is any color migration, pull the skein apart and soak it in Retyane®. Soak it for about 10 minutes, and then place it on some muslin to dry. If there is any color migration, do not use that color.

On a quilt made for a special occasion, like the birth of a child or a wedding, you may want to include a special note as to why the quilt was made and the special date.

If the recipient of the quilt might not know how to care for it, stitch a label with laundering instructions to the back.

HANGING QUILTS

The best way to hang a quilt is to sew a sleeve on the back. It should be shorter than the quilt's width by about 2". The finished width of the sleeve itself should be about 4".

Cut a strip of fabric 8" by the width of the quilt. Press the ends of the strip in about ½". Roll that ½" over another ½" and top stitch the folded edge (Fig. 44).

Fold the strip in half, right sides together, so it is now 4". Sew a ¼" seam allowance along the raw edges and turn the sleeve inside out. Position it on the back of the completed quilt about 1" from the top edge, and hand appliqué it in place.

You now need a dowel about 1" shorter than the width of your quilt, two finishing nails, and two eye screws from the hardware store. Most hardware stores will cut the dowel for you. Screw an eye screw, upright, ¼" to ½" from each end.

Hold the dowel on the wall and mark the opening of each of the eye screws. Place the finishing nails in the wall at these two marks. Put the dowel inside the sleeve and place the eye screws on the finishing nails.

If your quilt is wider than the longest dowel, use a lath board. This is a piece of wood about ¼" x 1". Leave an opening in the center of your sleeve and place a third eye screw in the center of the lath board. This will provide enough support so the quilt will hang straight and will not bow in the middle from the weight.

CLEANING QUILTS

I wash all of my quilts in Orvus® after they are completed. I use one to two tablespoons per quilt. If water in your area is soft, use less than one tablespoon; if it is hard, use two or more. Place the quilt in the washing machine, allow the machine to fill with water, and turn the machine off. Reach in and work the quilt with your hands. Allow the water to empty from the washer and fill it again, this time with no Orvus®. (This is the rinse water.) More than one rinse may be required. Keep rinsing until the water is clear. Drain all of the water and turn on the spin cycle. The force of the spin will remove much of the water.

Should the colors from one fabric in your project migrate onto another, keep the quilt wet. Then use Synthropal®, a chemical product marketed by Pro Chemical & Dye, Inc., and others. Try to keep the quilt wet, but even if it is dry, wash it with Synthropal®. Nothing is foolproof, but Synthropal® may save the quilt.

Drying

Lay quilts flat to dry. Do not dry the quilt in the dryer! When the fabric rubs on the dryer tub, it can become lighter because the color is brushed off. This is called "crocking."

There are at least two ways you can dry a quilt flat. You can lay it on a clean carpet (perhaps with a clean sheet under it). Depending on the type of batting, polyester will usually dry more quickly than cotton. If you wash a quilt in the evening, it will be dry when you get up in the morning. Using a fan in the room to help circulate the air will help speed the drying process. If the weather is clear, lay a clean sheet on the grass or decking area, lay the quilt on top of the sheet, and lay another clean sheet on top of the quilt. Anchor the corners with stones or bricks. Air circulation outdoors will quickly dry the quilt. Two things I do not recommend are dry cleaning and hanging a quilt to dry. Dry cleaning uses chemicals that may harm fabric and fade colors. Hanging a quilt may damage the quilting and sewing thread and cause the fabric to stretch. In addition, sunlight may fade fabric in a matter of minutes if a quilt is hung outdoors.

SECTION II

PROJECTS

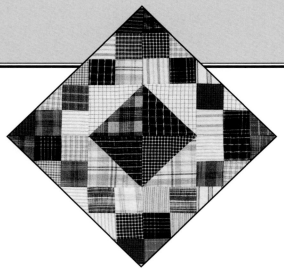

Scrap Happy

This project came about when the quilt guild in our area asked me to do something for a retreat weekend that would be fun, quick, and easy. This project meets all of those requirements. You need light and dark colors to contrast in order for the design to work well. Although the color photograph shows using plaids, scraps of any kind in light and dark will do the trick. What a great way to use up scraps so you can buy more fabric for something else!

The finished size of this piece is 64" x 64".

SUPPLIES

▶ Sewing machine
▶ Rotary cutter
▶ Cutting board
▶ Ruler
▶ Scissors
▶ Silk pins
▶ Thread to match

FABRICS

¼ yard each of 12 different dark prints
¼ yard each of 12 different light prints

Borders

2 yards for the borders and binding

Plate 1. SCRAP HAPPY, 64" x 64". Karen Kay Buckley

CUTTING INSTRUCTIONS

▶ Cut 144 – 2½" light fabric squares for the center portion of the wallhanging. If you would like do the border the same as the one in the photograph, you will need to cut an additional 54 – 2½" squares.

▶ Cut 144 – 2½" dark fabric squares for the center portion of the wallhanging. You will need an additional 54 squares for the border.

▶ Cut 36 – 4⅞" light fabric squares. Cut these into half-square triangles (Fig. 45).

▶ Cut 36 – 4⅞" dark fabric squares. Cut these into half-square triangles (Fig. 45).

SEWING INSTRUCTIONS

▶ Sew a light square to a dark square. You will need 144 of these units. Press the seams toward the darker fabric (Fig. 46).

▶ Sew the units into four-patch sections. Press in any direction (Fig. 47).

▶ Sew all of the dark triangles to a light triangle. Press toward the dark fabric. Press and sew gently. This seam is on the bias. Clip the tails. There are 36 of these units (Fig. 48).

▶ Sew a triangle square to a four-patch square and press the seams toward the four-patch. In order for the design to form, place the blocks as shown in Fig. 49.

▶ Sew the block to look like Fig. 50. Clip the center seam to allow you to press the seams toward the four-patch sections.

▶ Press all of the seams in the even-numbered rows in one direction and all of those in the odd-numbered rows in the opposite direction. Follow Fig. 51 for placement of the blocks and rows.

▶ Cut four strips 2½" x 55" long for the inner border.

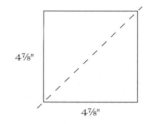

Fig. 45. Cutting half-square triangles.

Fig. 46. A light and dark square unit.

Fig. 47. A four-patch section.

Fig. 48. Press toward the dark fabric.

Fig. 49. Assembly diagram.

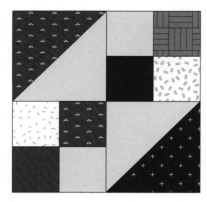

Fig. 50. The finished block.

▶ The 2½" squares you cut previously will be used for the pieced border. Sew 28 squares together, alternating light and dark for the sides. Sew 28 squares together for the top and bottom border area. See finished quilt, Plate 1, page 49.

▶ Cut the strips for the outer border 4½" wide and 68" long.

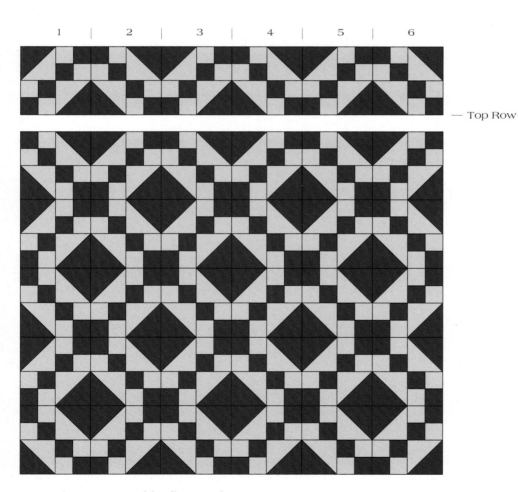

— Top Row

Fig. 51. Assembly diagram for SCRAP HAPPY.

NFL Stars

You might wonder how this quilt got its name. Well, I was trying to design a fun project to make for a class on Super Bowl Sunday! I love the diagonal design created by the dark squares. The quilt is much easier to piece than it looks. Fabric yardages are given for a lap or wall quilt and also for a bed quilt.

The center portion of this quilt is a 56" (76") square.

With borders cut as recommended, the quilt will finish into a 75" (96") square.

(The numbers in parentheses are for the bed quilt size.)

SUPPLIES

- ▶ Sewing machine
- ▶ Rotary cutter
- ▶ Cutting board
- ▶ Ruler to use with rotary cutter
- ▶ Thread to match
- ▶ Small piece of freezer paper (approximately 4" x 11")

FABRICS

1½ yards (2¼ yards) background (white)

1¼ yards (1½ yards) diagonal color (purple)

½ yard (1 yard) accent (burgundy)

1¼ yards (2 yards) color around stars (beige)

1 yard (1¼ yards) stars (dark green)

Borders

2 yards (3 yards) – center fabric

1 yard (1⅜ yards) if seamed

2¼ yards (3 yards) – inner border

1½ yards (2 yards) if seamed

2 yards (3 yards) accent, thin strips

¾ yard (1 yard) if seamed

½ yard (1 yard) binding

Plate 2. NFL STARS, 75" x 75". Karen Kay Buckley

CUTTING INSTRUCTIONS

FABRIC #1 – BACKGROUND (WHITE):

▶ Cut 8 (12) strips 2½" wide.

▶ Cut 4 (7) strips 5¼" wide. Cut these into 5¼" squares. Cut the squares on both diagonals (Fig. 52a). You will need 120 (224) of these quarter-square triangles.

FABRIC #2 – DIAGONAL COLOR (PURPLE):

▶ Cut 2 (3) strips 4½" wide. Cut these into 4½" squares. You will need 12 (24) of these squares.

▶ Cut 10 (12) strips 2½" wide.

FABRIC #3 – ACCENT (BURGUNDY):

▶ Cut 2 (4) strips 5¼" wide. Cut these into 5¼" squares. Cut these squares on both diagonals. You will need 60 (112) of these triangles (Fig. 52a).

FABRIC #4 – COLOR AROUND STARS (BEIGE):

▶ Cut 5 (8) strips 2½" wide.

▶ Cut 5 (10) strips 3¾". Make three freezer paper templates using Template A, page 56. Iron the freezer paper templates to the strip and cut around the freezer paper adding a ¼" seam allowance on all sides. Repeat for a total of 60 (112) squares.

FABRIC #5 – STARS (DARK GREEN):

▶ Cut 2 (3) strips 4½" wide. Cut these into 4½" squares. You will need 13 (25) of these squares.

▶ Cut 5 (8) strips 2⅞" wide. Cut these into 2⅞" squares. Cut these into half-square triangles. You will need 120 (224) of these triangles (Fig. 52b).

Borders

Based on the yardage given, the width of the borders are the same regardless of the size you are doing. The length will be different based on the yardage you purchased.

▶ Cut inner and outer borders 3".

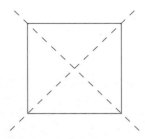

Fig. 52a. Cut the squares into quarter-square triangles.

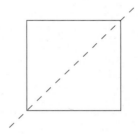

Fig. 52b. Cut the half-square triangle in half.

Fig. 53. Assemble three colors, 2½" strips, together. Press away from the center strips.

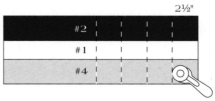

Fig. 54. The strips are cut into sections or units. See general instructions for complete rotary cutting instructions.

Fig. 55. Sew these three strips together to form a long group.

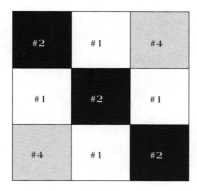

Fig. 56. Assembly diagram for nine-patch block.

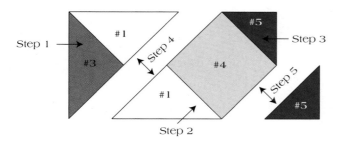

Fig. 57. Assembly diagram for the NFL Stars sections.

▶ Cut middle border 3½".

▶ Cut accent border 1½".

SEWING INSTRUCTIONS

▶ To assemble the block, sew three 2½" strips together. Sew a #2, #1, and #4, with the #1 in the center. Press the seams away from #1 (Fig. 53).

▶ Cut these strips into 2½" sections (Fig. 54). You will need 72 (128) of these units. You should get approximately 17 units per group of strips, so you will need 5 (8) groups of these strips.

▶ Sew another set of three 2½" strips together. This time join #1, #2, and #1, with the #2 fabric in the center (Fig. 55). Also cut these into 2½" sections. You will need 36 (64) of these units. Note: you might be able to get all of these from the 2 (4) long groups, but you may need to sew an additional small group to get the number you need. It will depend on the width of the fabric.

▶ Sew the 2½" sections together into nine-patch blocks (Fig. 56). Because the seams are pressed in opposite directions you should not need any pins. Be careful on your color placement. You will need 36 (64) of these nine-patch units.

▶ Refer to Fig. 57 and the following steps to complete the alternate sections.

1. Sew a background #1 triangle to an accent #3 triangle. Be sure you are sewing these in the correct direction. Press the seams toward the accent triangle.

2. Sew a background #1 triangle to a #4 square. Press the seam toward the square. Remember to be careful of the direction.

3. Sew a star fabric #5 triangle to the oppo-

site side of the #4 square. Press the seam toward the square.

4. Sew step 1 to 2 to 3. Press the seams toward step 1 (Fig. 58).

5. Sew a star fabric #5 triangle to the bottom of this unit. Press the seams toward the star triangle.

▶ You will need 60 (112) of these units.

▶ Refer to the layout for the size quilt you have selected. As you are sewing the units together, be sure the points from the alternate units meet the seam on the nine-patch blocks. You might want to pin this point. As you sew the rows together, watch those stars shine!

Fig. 58. Assembly diagram for row.

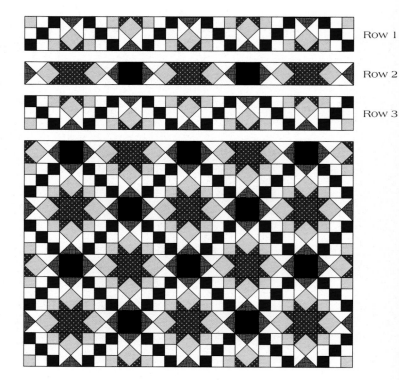

Row 1

Row 2

Row 3

Fig. 59a. Layout and placement diagram for NFL STARS quilt. Join together by rows.

NFL STARS TEMPLATE A

Template A, NFL STARS quilt.

Lap/Wall

Lap/Wall

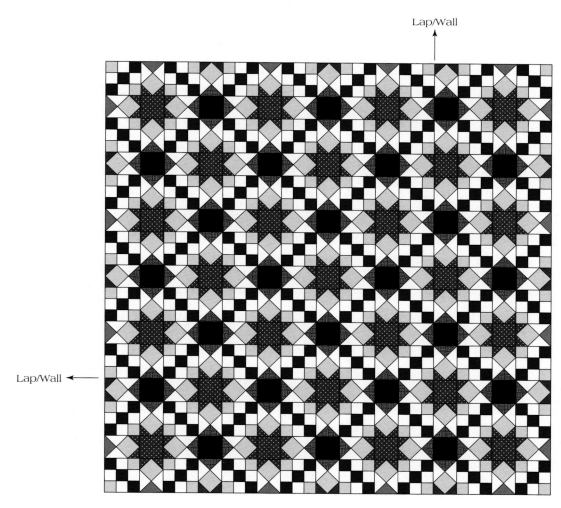

Fig. 59b. Layout and placement diagram for
NFL STARS lap/wall and bed quilt.

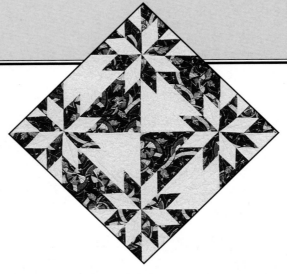

Hunter's Star

This pattern has always appealed to me because stars form in each corner where the blocks meet. The hardest part of this project is choosing only two fabrics. The choices are endless. The only thing you need to be concerned with is that there is a strong contrast between the two fabrics you choose.

The finished size of this piece is 54" x 68".

SUPPLIES

- ▶ Fabric markers
- ▶ Ruler
- ▶ Rotary cutter
- ▶ Cutting board
- ▶ Sewing machine
- ▶ Template plastic
- ▶ Silk pins
- ▶ Thread to match
- ▶ Paper scissors

FABRICS

2½ yards of one fabric

2½ yards of a contrasting second fabric

2 yards for the border

¾ yard for binding

Plate 3. HUNTER'S STAR, 54" x 68". Karen Kay Buckley

CUTTING INSTRUCTIONS

▶ Make the diamonds by cutting eight 2" strips from each fabric. Position your ruler with the 45° angle on top of the strip and rotary cut 2" diamonds. You need 96 light and 96 dark diamonds. (Refer to the section about rotary cutting diamonds, page 20).

▶ Make the triangles by cutting four strips at 5⅞" from each fabric and rotary cutting these into half-square triangles. You need 48 light and 48 dark triangles (Fig. 60).

▶ Make a template of the trapezoid shape (Template A, page 61). Take your time and be sure it is accurate.

▶ Cut eight 2" strips. Use the template and a pencil to mark the fabric. Place the trapezoid right side up and then upside down. Cut on the 45° lines, and then cut off the points. This will ensure accurate and easier piecing later. You need 48 light and 48 dark trapezoids. (Fig. 61).

SEWING INSTRUCTIONS

▶ Sew a contrasting diamond to each side of a trapezoid. Make sure the side of the diamond lines up with the corner of the trapezoid (Fig. 62).

▶ Sew a dark diamond to each side of a light trapezoid and sew a light diamond to each side of a dark trapezoid. Press the seams toward the darker fabric and clip the tails (Fig. 63).

▶ Sew these units together. Because the seams of these units are pressed toward the darker fabrics, you should not need to pin the seams. The seams should automatically butt. Press these sewn seams toward the darker diamonds.

▶ Center and sew a triangle to each side of the previous unit (Fig. 64). Press toward

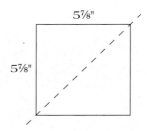

Fig. 60. Cutting half-square triangles.

Fig. 61. Layout and cutting diagram for marking template pieces. Trim off points.

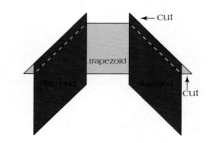

Fig. 62.

Fig. 63. Assemble units together. Sewn seams are pressed toward diamonds.

Fig. 64. A finished block measures 7½" x 7½" with seam allowances.

the darker fabric. These blocks should measure 7½" x 7½", with the seam allowance.

▶ Sew the blocks in rows, pinning to line up the seams between the rows and across the rows (Fig. 65, page 62).

▶ Cut border strips 6" wide. See photograph of quilt, page 59.

▶ Use the template on page 63 to mark quilting lines on the border.

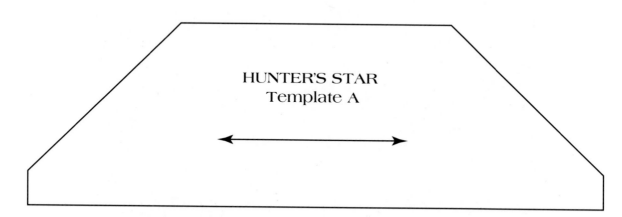

HUNTER'S STAR
Template A

Template A, HUNTER'S STAR quilt. Includes seam allowance.

Fig. 65. Assembly diagram for HUNTER'S STAR
quilt. Join the blocks into rows by alternating
colors. Note: Dotted lines show quilting design.

QUILTING

▶ Make a plastic template of the outer solid lines of the pattern. The dotted lines on the border can be drawn with your ruler.

▶ Quilt along both solid and dotted lines.

▶ Quilt 8-point stars into the border area.

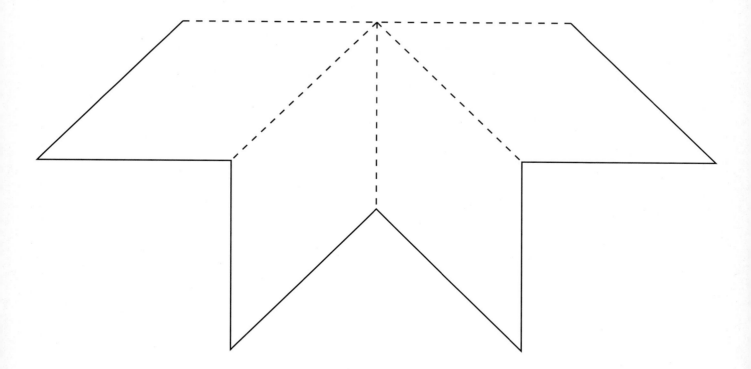

Quilting pattern, HUNTER'S STAR quilt.

Irish Stars

The Irish Chain pattern has always been one of my favorites as have most star patterns, so combining the two seemed natural. Consider making the border wider or adding another border to the outside edge if you want the quilt a little larger. Yardage is given for a bed quilt size and a lap throw.

The finished size of this piece is 65¼" x 87¾".

Bed quilt finished size is 78¾" x 101¼".

(The numbers in parentheses are for the bed size quilt.)

SUPPLIES

▶ Sewing machine

▶ Rotary cutter

▶ Cutting board

▶ Ruler to use with rotary cutter

▶ Thread to match

FABRICS

1 yard (2 yards) (my white)

2½ yards (3⅜ yards) for border and blocks (my green)

2 yards (3⅜ yards) (my blue)

2⅜ yards (4⅛ yards) (my purple)

1 yard (1¼ yard) for binding

Plate 4. IRISH STARS, 65¼" x 87¾". Karen Kay Buckley

CUTTING INSTRUCTIONS

FABRIC #1 – WHITE:

▶ Cut 16 (33) strips 1¾" wide.

FABRIC #2 – GREEN:

▶ Cut four border strips 4½" (5") wide by the length of your fabric. Use the remaining fabric to complete the cutting for the blocks.

▶ Cut 20 (34) strips 1¾" wide.

FABRIC #3 – BLUE:

▶ Cut 3 (7) strips 1¾" wide.

▶ Cut 6 (10) strips 5" wide. Cut these strips into squares and cut the squares into quarter-square triangles (Fig. 66). You will need 184 (312) of these triangles.

▶ Cut 3 (4) strips 9¼" wide. Cut these into 11¾" sections. You need 7 (12) of these sections.

▶ For the lap throw size you will have enough of your 9¼" wide strip left over to use for the piecing of the alternate blocks. However, for the larger sizes you will need to cut 1 strip 9¼" wide. Do not cut this into anything smaller.

FABRIC #4 – PURPLE:

▶ Cut 6 (10) strips 5" wide. Cut these into squares and cut the squares into quarter-square triangles (Fig. 66). You need 184 (312) of these triangles.

▶ Cut 9 (13) strips 1¾" wide.

▶ Cut 7 (19) strips 3" wide.

▶ Cut 1 (1) strip 9¼" wide. For the larger size, you may need a little more; it depends on the width of your fabrics. You can cut more later if needed.

SEWING INSTRUCTIONS

▶ To begin assembling the block, sew the 1¾" wide fabric pieces #1, #2, and #1 together with #2 in the center. Press the seams toward fabric #2. You will need 3

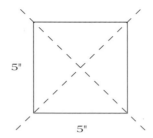

Fig. 66. Cut squares into quarter-square triangles.

Fig. 67. Cut the strips into sections after joining by color.

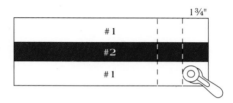

Fig. 68. The sewn and cut section is called a unit.

Fig. 69. Assembly diagram.

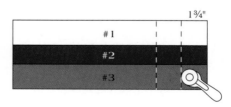

Fig. 70. These strips will form the corner units.

Fig. 71. Assembly diagram.

Fig. 72. These squares will form the corner units.

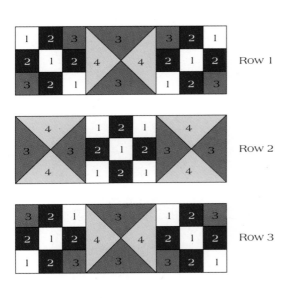

Row 1

Row 2

Row 3

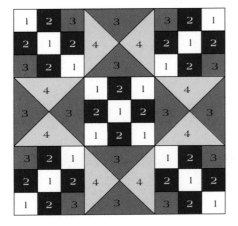

Fig. 73. Three rows combined to make Block A.

(4) of these groups. Cut these into 1¾" sections (Fig. 67). You need 56 (78) of these units.

▶ Sew another set of 1¾" strips together. Join two #2 strips with a #1 strip in the center. Press the seams toward fabric #2. You need 5 (8) of these groups. Cut these into 1¾" sections (Fig. 68). You need 100 (174) of these units.

▶ Use some of the units from above to complete the blocks shown in Figure 69. Some of these units will be used later for the border blocks. If the seams have been pressed correctly, butt the seams and do not use pins. Press the seams toward the center. You will need 28 (46) of these blocks.

▶ To make the corner units for the inside stars, sew strips of fabric #1 and #2 to a #3, with the #2 in the center. Cut these into 1¾" sections (Fig. 70). You will need 64 (144) of these units.

▶ You need to make 32 (72) of these nine-patch units as shown in Figure 71 for the corners of the stars. Press the seams toward the center. These blocks will be used in the center portion of the quilt.

▶ Sew the triangles cut from the 5" squares into units as shown in Figure 72. Sew a #3 to a #4. Press the seams toward the #4 fabric. Sew the long seam down the center. Press the seam in either direction and clip the tails. You need 92 (156) of these units.

▶ For the center portion of the quilt you will need 8 (18) of the blocks shown in Figure 73. Press the seams toward the nine-patch sections. We will refer to these as Block A.

▶ To make the alternate blocks for the center portion of the quilt, sew a fabric #2 –

1¾" wide strip to each side of a fabric #3 – 9¼" wide strip (Fig. 74a). Cut these into 1¾" wide sections. You need 14 (24) of these sections.

▶ Sew one of the previous units to each side of a 9¼" x 11¾" piece from fabric #3 (Fig. 74b). You need 7 (12) of these blocks.

▶ Press the seams toward the side units. These will be referred to as Block B.

▶ You are now ready to make the star blocks for the outer section. These will be called Block C. These blocks are made the same as the center blocks. The only difference is color placement.

▶ Sew together the cut 1¾" strips #1, #2, and #4 with the #2 fabric in the center. You will need to make 4 (5) of these groups. Cut these into 1¾" sections (Fig. 75). You need 80 (112) of these units.

▶ Several of the units you made previously will now be used to complete Block C.

▶ Make Block C by referring to Figure 76. You need 10 (14) of these blocks. Press the seams toward the nine-patch units.

▶ To make Block D, sew fabric #2 – 1¾" wide strip to a 9¼" wide fabric #4. Press the seams toward fabric #2. Cut these into 1¾" sections (Fig. 77). You will need 20 (28) of these units. You will get all of these units from one group for the lap throw, but you will need to make an additional small group to complete the 28 needed for the larger bed quilt size.

▶ Sew Block D as shown in Figure 78. You will need 10 (14) of these blocks.

▶ Refer to the layout diagrams for placement of the blocks (Figures 79a and b, pages 70 and 71).

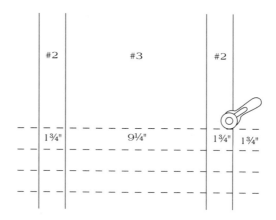

Fig. 74a. Assemble, sew, and cut these strips into sections.

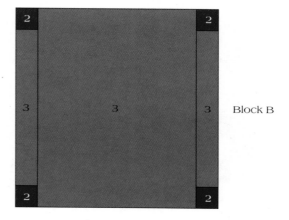

Fig. 74b. The sections are attached to form Block B.

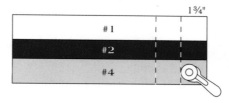

Fig. 75. Cut the strips into sections after joining by color.

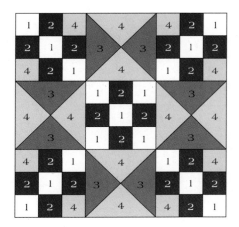

Block C

Fig. 76. Assembly diagram for Block C.

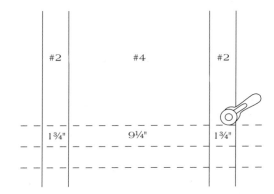

#2   #4   #2

1¾"   9¼"   1¾"

Fig. 77. Units cut from one group of colored pieces.

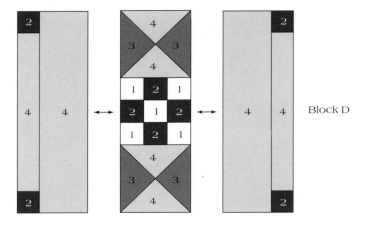

Block D

Fig. 78. Units cut from one group of colored pieces.

Fig. 79a. Layout diagram for IRISH STARS lap throw.

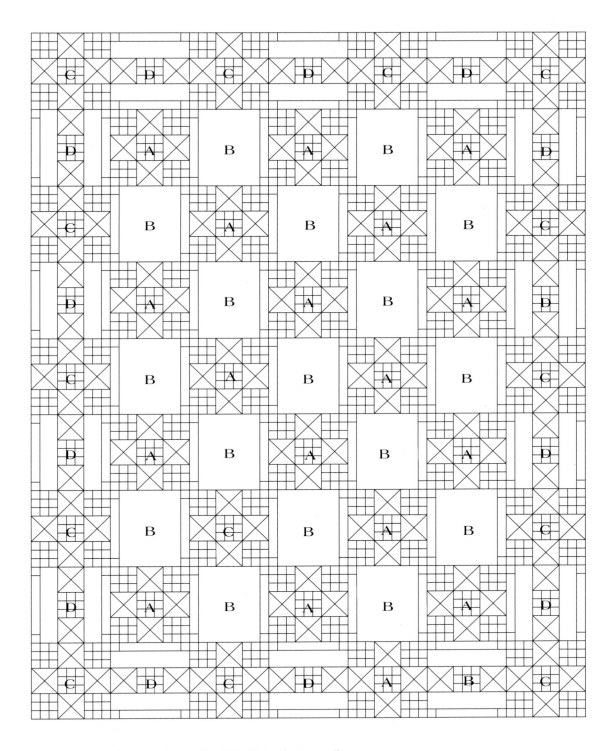

Fig. 79b. Layout diagram for IRISH STARS bed size quilt.

Trip Around the Flower Garden

This wonderful little wall quilt combines regular appliqué, some reverse appliqué, and quick and easy pieced corners. Because of its size it goes quickly and would make a nice gift. It is especially quick if you machine appliqué and machine quilt it!

The finished size of this piece is 31" x 31".

SUPPLIES

- ▸ Appliqué supplies of your choice
- ▸ Marking tools for appliqué placement
- ▸ Rotary cutter
- ▸ Cutting board
- ▸ Ruler to use with rotary cutter
- ▸ Thread for piecing and appliqué
- ▸ Bias Press Bars®

FABRICS

I recommend using four shades of one color (rose) and three shades of another color (blue).

⅛ yard fabric #1: lightest of the four-shades group (rose)

⅛ yard fabric #2: second lightest of the four-shades group (rose)

⅛ yard fabric #3: medium of the four-shades group (rose)

¼ yard fabric #4: darkest of the four-shades group (rose)

¼ yard fabric #5: lightest of the three-shades group (blue)

¼ yard fabric #6: medium of the three-shades group (blue)

¼ yard fabric #7: darkest of the three-shades group (blue)

⅝ yard for border and binding (I recommend fabric #7)

⅝ yard for background fabric – light print

Plate 5. TRIP AROUND THE FLOWER GARDEN, 31" x 31". Karen Kay Buckley

CUTTING INSTRUCTIONS

All of the squares below are to be cut 1¾", unless otherwise noted. These small 1¾" squares will be used for the corner units.

FABRIC #1 – LIGHTEST OF FOUR-SHADES GROUP

▸ Cut 1 D appliqué flower piece and 16 squares

FABRIC #2 – SECOND LIGHTEST OF FOUR-SHADES GROUP

▸ Cut 4 F pieces and 20 squares

FABRIC #3 – MEDIUM OF FOUR-SHADES GROUP

▸ Cut 28 squares

FABRIC #4 – DARKEST OF FOUR-SHADES GROUP

▸ Cut 1 C flower, 4 G small flower pieces, and 36 squares

FABRIC #5 – LIGHTEST OF THE THREE-SHADES GROUP

▸ Cut 16 K pieces and 44 squares

FABRIC #6 – MEDIUM OF THE THREE-SHADES GROUP

▸ Cut 16 K pieces and 52 squares

FABRIC #7 – DARKEST OF THE THREE-SHADES GROUP

▸ Cut 14 3" squares. Cut these into quarter-square triangles (Fig. 80). You will need 56 of these triangles.

▸ Also from fabric #7, cut 2 squares 1¾" and cut these into half-square triangles (Fig. 81). You will need 4 of these triangles.

▸ See appliqué pieces for more cutting instructions.

Appliqué Pieces:

▸ See pages 24–31 for complete appliqué sewing advice and page 20 for pressing information.

▸ Cut a 21" x 21" square from the background fabric. This is slightly larger than needed, which will allow you to trim it to the exact size when the appliqué is completed.

▸ Transfer the appliqué design to your background fabric.

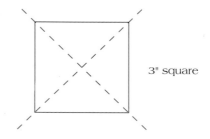

3" square

Fig. 80. Cut 3" squares into quarter triangles.

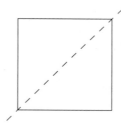

Fig. 81. Cut square into half-square triangles.

fabric

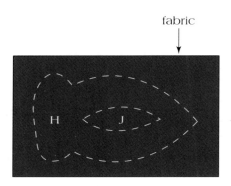

Fig. 82a. Trace the flower bud pattern H onto the fabric. Dotted lines indicate edges of pattern and will be sewing lines.

slit and clip into seams

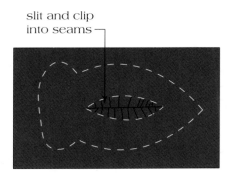

Fig. 82b. Cut a slit in the marked opening (J), clip into the seam allowance.

trim seam allowance

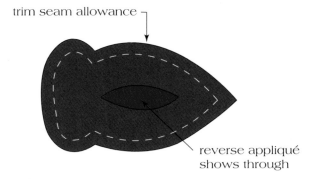

reverse appliqué
shows through

Fig. 82c. Trim seam allowance around shape after opening is sewn and pressed.

▶ The shapes are lettered in the order of placement. The short stems must be appliquéd first. When the longer B stems are appliquéd, they will cover the raw edges on the bottom of stem A. The short A stems are made using the ¼" Bias Press Bar®. The strips need to be cut 1½" wide and they need to be cut on the bias. Be sure the ends of the stems extend ¼" into the next shape so their raw edges will be covered when the next shape is appliquéd.

▶ The long B stems are made using the ⅜" Bias Press Bar® (see page 31). The bias strips should be cut 1½" wide.

▶ Following the instructions on page 32, make a circle for the center E shape, using a quarter as your template.

▶ To complete the reverse appliqué in the center of the H flower shape. Use the remaining scraps of fabric #7. Trace the H flower bud shape onto the right side of your fabric (Fig. 82a). Be sure to trace the opening, also. Cut a rectangular shape, but do not cut the seam allowance yet. With a small pair of sharp-pointed scissors, cut a slit in the opening. Clip into the seam allowance (Fig. 82b).

▶ Place a small rectangular piece of fabric #4 under the opening of the H shape. Pin the layers together. Appliqué stitch the edges of the opening and the J shape in the lighter color will show through the H shape. Now cut a seam allowance around the H flower bud shape and appliqué it in place (Fig. 82c).

▶ Repeat for seven more buds.

▶ Sew the corner units by referring to Figure 83, page 76. Be sure to sew with a ¼" seam allowance. Press the seams in

Harrison Rose

This is a nice little wallhanging, perfect for gift giving or the right spot in your home. The gentle soft curves of this traditional appliqué pattern, combined with these pretty colors, make this a very soothing piece to quilt and admire.

The finished size of this piece is 34" x 34".

SUPPLIES

- ▸ Supplies for the appliqué method of your choice
- ▸ Thread to match your appliqué and piecing fabrics
- ▸ Bias Press Bars®
- ▸ Fabric scissors
- ▸ Paper scissors
- ▸ Ruler
- ▸ Silk pins

FABRICS

¼ yard green fabric for stems and leaves

⅛ yard of a second green for leaves

¼ yard of one fabric for the flowers in the center and border area (my navy blue)

1 yard for the background

1 yard for the corner border sections, appliqué, and binding (flower print)

¾ yard for the outer border and inner border area, includes enough for the appliqué and binding (my rose)

1⅛ yard for backing

Plate 6. HARRISON ROSE, 34" x 34". Karen Kay Buckley

CUTTING INSTRUCTIONS

FROM THE BACKGROUND FABRIC: – WHITE/CREAM

- ▶ Cut 1 – 20" square for the center
- ▶ Cut 4 – 4½" x 11½" rectangles for the border

FROM THE CORNER BORDER FABRIC: (my flower print)

- ▶ Cut 8 – 4½" x 11" strips. This allows a little extra to make the miter.
- ▶ Cut 4 – 2" wide strips for the binding
- ▶ Cut 4 – D pieces for appliqué

FROM THE INNER AND OUTER BORDER FABRIC: (my rose)

- ▶ Cut 4 – 2" wide strips for the outer border
- ▶ Cut 2 – 2" wide strips for the inner border. Cut these in half so you will have four inner border strips.
- ▶ Cut 8 – B pieces for appliqué
- ▶ Cut 8 – C pieces for appliqué
- ▶ Cut 1 – E piece for appliqué

FROM THE ¼ YARD FLOWER APPLIQUÉ FABRIC: (my navy blue)

- ▶ Cut 1 – F piece for appliqué
- ▶ Cut 8 – B pieces for appliqué
- ▶ Cut 8 – C pieces for appliqué

FROM THE ¼ YARD GREEN FABRIC:

- ▶ Cut 32 – A pieces for leaves
- ▶ Cut several strips 1¼" wide, on the bias, to be used for stems.

FROM THE ⅛ YARD SECOND GREEN FABRIC:

- ▶ Cut 16 – A pieces for appliqué

SEWING INSTRUCTIONS

- ▶ Transfer the appliqué design (Pattern 1-1 and 1-2) to your 20" background square. Appliqué the stems first. Then appliqué each shape, in the order they are lettered. Refer to Section 1.
- ▶ Transfer the appliqué design (Pattern 1-0) to the 4½" x 11½" border sections. Appliqué the stems first. Then appliqué the flowers and leaves in the order they are lettered.
- ▶ Sew a 4½" x 11" border fabric to each end of the 4½" x 11½" appliqué border design (Fig. 84). Sew all four borders together so they can be mitered at one time. Be sure to center the appliqué design between the inner and outer border strips.
- ▶ Attach each of the four borders to a side of the center portion and miter the corners.
- ▶ Bind the quilt.

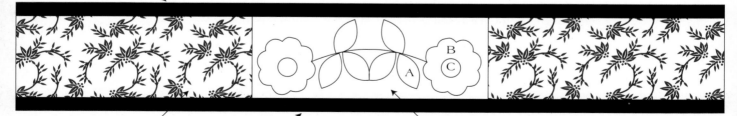

2" outer border

4½" x 11" corner border   2" inner border   Placement guide for appliqué design

Fig. 84. Assembly diagram for appliquéd and pieced borders. Shown before mitering corners.

Placement guide for appliqué design on borders of quilt.

PATTERN 1-0, for appliqué borders, HARRISON ROSE quilt. Full size pattern. Add seam allowances.

Complete placement diagram for the HARRISON
ROSE appliquéd center.

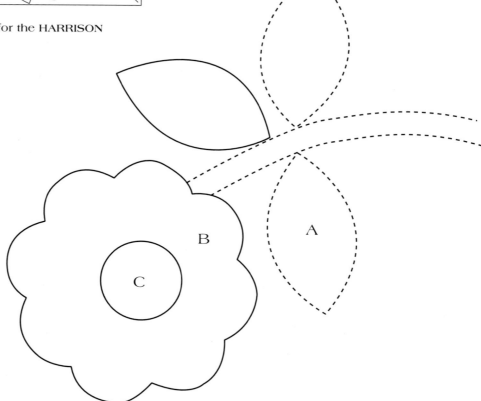

PATTERN 1-1, for appliqué block center, HARRI-
SON ROSE quilt. Full size pattern. Add seam
allowances. Overlap to next page.

PATTERN 1-2, for appliqué block center, HARRISON ROSE quilt. Dotted lines show ¼ of design. Full size pattern pieces. Add seam allowances. Connect four repeats.

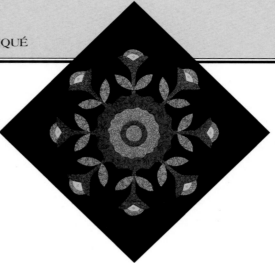

Rose Trellis

This is a very sophisticated looking wallhanging, but it is very easy to complete. Wouldn't this look great hanging in your home over the sofa, or the fireplace? It would also be a wonderful wedding gift or anniversary present.

The finished size of this piece is 49" x 49".

SUPPLIES

- ▸ Supplies for the appliqué method of your choice
- ▸ Fabric markers
- ▸ Fabric scissors
- ▸ Paper scissors
- ▸ Cutting board
- ▸ Rotary cutter
- ▸ Ruler
- ▸ Silk pins
- ▸ Sewing machine

FABRICS

2⅛ yards for the background

½ yard for the inner border and appliqué (medium pink)

1½ yards green for the lattice border and appliqué

⅜ yard dark pink

¼ yard light green

⅛ yard light pink

2¾ yards for the backing

⅜ yard for binding

Plate 7. ROSE TRELLIS, 49" x 49". Karen Kay Buckley

CUTTING INSTRUCTIONS

FROM THE BACKGROUND FABRIC:

▶ Cut a square 23" for the center background section. This measurement includes a seam allowance.

▶ Cut two 20" squares to be cut into half-square triangles. Before cutting these, draw a center diagonal line, and stitch approximately ⅛" on each side of the line. (Fig. 85). Since these long sides of the triangle are on the bias, the ⅛" stitch line will keep them from stretching. It really does help. The reason for stitching them ⅛" is because when you sew with a ¼" seam allowance, the ⅛" will be lost in the seam and you will never need to remove those stitches. These will be your four corner triangles (Fig. 86).

▶ Cut four strips 6½" x 40". These will be used for the lattice border. (This includes a little extra length, in case it's needed.)

▶ Cut four 6½" squares for the corners of the border.

FROM THE GREEN FABRIC:

▶ Cut strips for the lattice 1½" wide and 10" long. You will need 120 of these strips.

MAKE TEMPLATES FOR APPLIQUÉ PIECES A THROUGH J.

FOR APPLIQUÉ CUT THE FOLLOWING PIECES:

8	A pieces	(inner border fabric)
8	B pieces	(light pink)
8	C pieces	(green for lattice and appliqué)
16	D pieces	(inner border fabric)
16	E pieces	(light green)
1	F piece	(dark pink)
1	G piece	(inner border fabric)
1	H piece	(dark pink)
1	J piece	(inner border fabric)

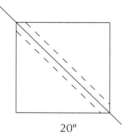

Fig. 85.

Fig. 86.

Fig. 87.

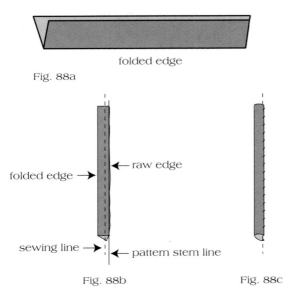

folded edge

Fig. 88a

folded edge → ← raw edge

sewing line → ← pattern stem line

Fig. 88b   Fig. 88c

Fig. 88a, b, and c. Prepare the fabric for straight grain appliqué by folding in half. Stitch ¼" from edge, press over and appliqué the folded edge.

▶ Transfer the appliqué design (Patterns 2-0, 2-1, and 2-2) to the background fabric using the placement guide (page 88).

▶ Appliqué the pieces in the order they are lettered. After the center appliqué section is complete, add the inner border. Then add the four corner triangles (Fig. 86).

▶ The last step will be to sew the lattice outer border area. Since these are straight sections, they can be cut on the grain and do not need to be cut on the bias. Draw a line down the center of each lattice border strip. This will be 3¼". Lattice lines will be on a 45° angle. The lines should meet in the center on the 3¼" line. Starting 1⅜" from the edge, draw a line every 2" until the entire surface of the border fabric is filled (Fig. 87).

▶ Press all of the green lattice strips in half, wrong sides together (Fig. 88a). Place the raw edge of the strip on the lines you drew and sew ¼" from the raw edge (Fig. 88b). Press the strip over (Fig. 88c) and appliqué the folded edge in place.

▶ Do all of the strips in one direction, and then do all of the strips in the other direction. Sew a lattice border to each side of the center section. Attempt to have the lattice center meet the point on the inner border (Fig. 89).

▶ Sew a 6½" background square to each end of a lattice strip. Sew these to the top and bottom.

▶ Quilt and bind.

meet at point

Fig. 89.

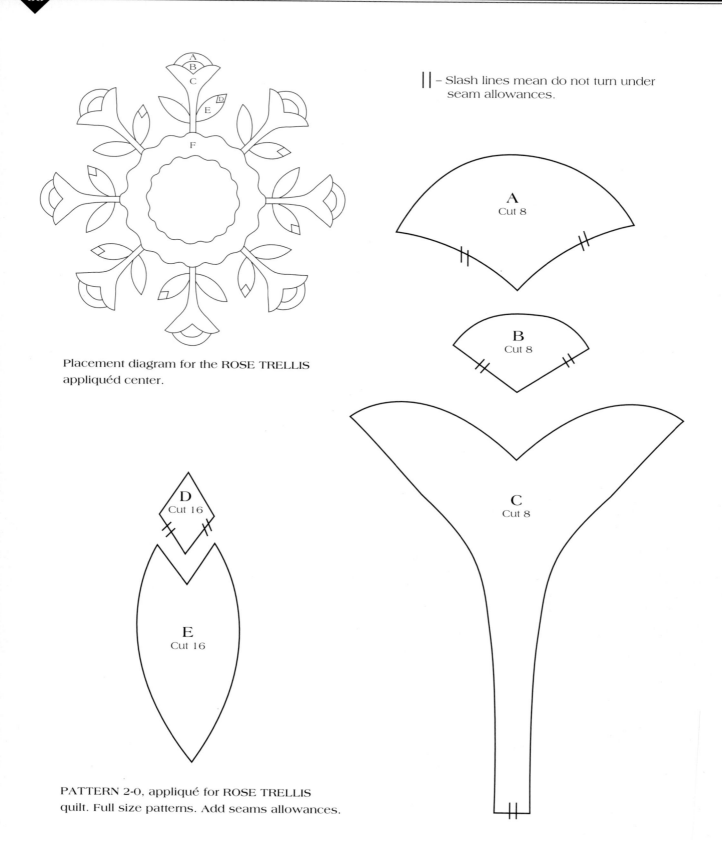

|| – Slash lines mean do not turn under
seam allowances.

Placement diagram for the ROSE TRELLIS
appliquéd center.

A
Cut 8

B
Cut 8

C
Cut 8

D
Cut 16

E
Cut 16

PATTERN 2-0, appliqué for ROSE TRELLIS
quilt. Full size patterns. Add seams allowances.

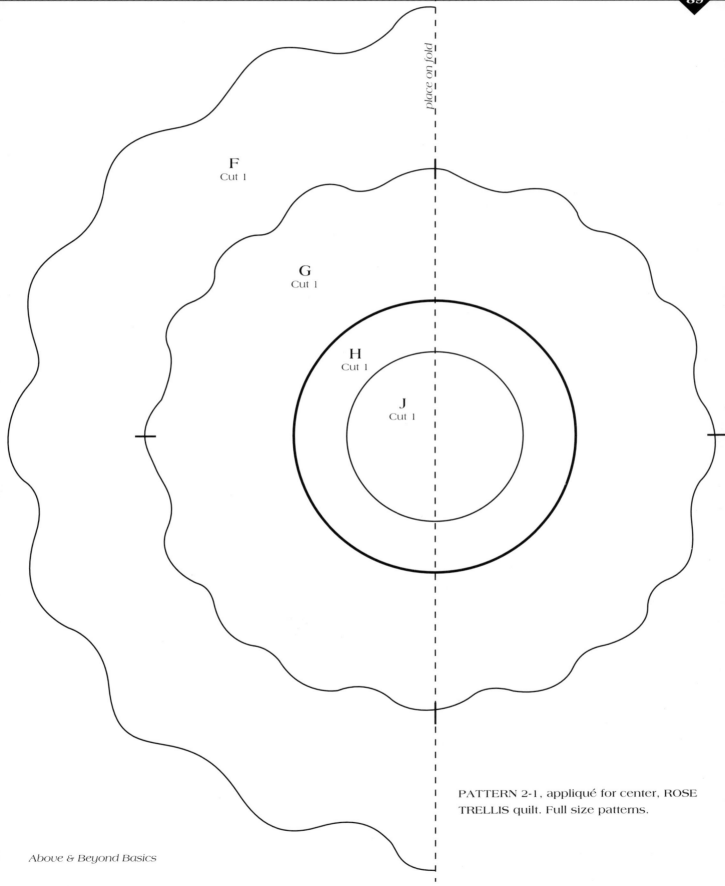

place on fold

F
Cut 1

G
Cut 1

H
Cut 1

J
Cut 1

PATTERN 2-1, appliqué for center, ROSE
TRELLIS quilt. Full size patterns.

Placement diagram for the ROSE TRELLIS
appliquéd center.

E

PATTERN 2-2, appliqué for center, ROSE
TRELLIS quilt. Full size patterns.

A

B

C

D

E

F

G

PATTERN 2-2, appliqué for center, ROSE
TRELLIS quilt. Full size patterns. Full size pattern. Add seam allowances. Overlap with pro-
ceeding page. Connect four repeats.

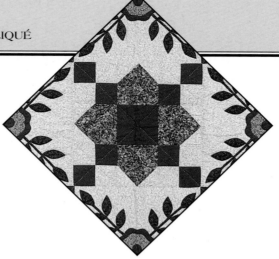

Down the Garden Path

Don't you just love this combination? The diagonal lines formed by the appliqué and the pieced blocks make this quilt move. Measurements for a wallhanging size and a double bed quilt are given.

The finished size of this piece as a double bed quilt is 80" x 80".

The finished size of the wallhanging is 54" x 54".

(The numbers in the parentheses are for wallhanging.)

SUPPLIES

▶ Supplies for the appliqué method of your choice
▶ Cutting board
▶ Rotary cutter
▶ Ruler
▶ Sewing machine
▶ Silk pins
▶ Thread to match for piecing and appliqué

FABRICS

1 yard (½ yard) burgundy
¼ yard (⅛ yard) pink
1 yard (½ yard) flower print
2½ yards (1¼ yard) light print
1¾ yards (¾ yard) green
2½ yards (1¾ yard) burgundy for borders
2¼ yard (1⅝ yard) light print for borders
1 yard (⅜ yard) for binding
5 yards (3¼ yard) for backing

Plate 8. DOWN THE GARDEN PATH, 80" x 80". Karen Kay Buckley

CUTTING INSTRUCTIONS

FROM THE BURGUNDY FABRIC CUT THE FOLLOWING:
(THE NUMBERS IN PARENTHESES ARE FOR THE WALL-HANGING.)

- ▶ 2 (1) strips 4½" wide, cut into squares. You need 13 (5) squares.
- ▶ 7 (2) strips 2½" wide. These will be used for the four-patch sections.
- ▶ 12 (4) small 1" circles (E)
- ▶ 12 (4) large flowers (C)

FROM THE FLOWER PRINT CUT THE FOLLOWING:

- ▶ 4 (2) strips 2⅞" wide, cut into squares, and then cut into half-square triangles (Fig. 90). You will need 104 (40) squares.
- ▶ 6 (3) strips 2½", cut into rectangles 4½". You need 52 (20) rectangles.

FROM THE LIGHT PRINT CUT THE FOLLOWING:

- ▶ 7 (2) strips 2½", for the four-patch sections.
- ▶ 4 (2) strips 2⅞", cut into squares, and then cut into half-square triangles (Fig. 90). You will need 104 (40).
- ▶ 12 (4) 12½" squares

FROM THE GREEN FOR STEMS AND LEAVES CUT THE FOLLOWING:

- ▶ 6 (2) strips ¾" wide for the stems (A), cut on grain.
- ▶ 240 (80) leaves (B)

FROM THE BURGUNDY FABRIC CUT THE FOLLOWING:

- ▶ Cut 2½" (2") wide strips for the border

FROM THE LIGHT PRINT CUT THE FOLLOWING:

- ▶ Cut 6" (5") wide strips for the inner border.

SEWING INSTRUCTIONS

- ▶ Sew each of the burgundy 2½" strips to a 2½" light print strip. Press the seams toward the darker fabric.
- ▶ Cut these strips into 2½" sections (Fig. 91).
- ▶ Sew these sections into four-patch units. Carefully match the intersections.
- ▶ To complete the next unit, sew triangle

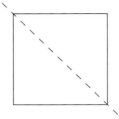

Fig. 90. Cut strips into 2⅞" squares and then into half-square triangles.

Fig. 91. Press seams toward the darker colored fabric when joining strips together, then cut into 2½" sections.

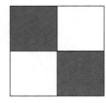

Fig. 92. Assembly diagram for the four-patch units.

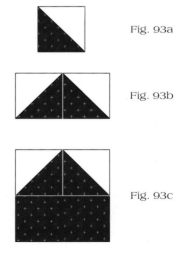

Fig. 93a

Fig. 93b

Fig. 93c

Fig. 93a, b, and c. Assemble two triangle units into a point and attach a rectangle base to form a new piece.

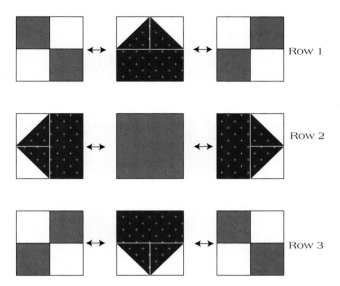

Fig. 94. Join the patchwork block by rows. Carefully follow this placement diagram.

folded edge

Fig. 95. Prepare the fabric for straight-grain appliquéd stems by folding in half.

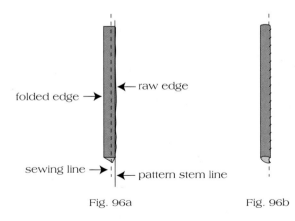

folded edge →
← raw edge

sewing line →
← pattern stem line

Fig. 96a   Fig. 96b

Fig. 96a and b. Stitching diagram for attaching green stems. Use appliqué stitch.

units together (Fig. 93a). (These are the half-square triangles from the 2⅞" squares.)

▶ Sew two of these units together so they come to a point (Fig. 93b).

▶ Sew a rectangle to the bottom of each of these units (Fig. 93c). Press the seams toward the triangles.

▶ Assemble the patchwork block as in Figure 94. After pressing, you'll see that the triangles have a tail that extends past the raw edge of the fabric. Clip these tails to remove the excess fabric. It will make it easier to match the block when sewing these pieces to the others in the quilt.

▶ Transfer the appliqué design to the 12½" background squares. Appliqué the shapes in the order they are lettered. The stems, A, are appliquéd first. Because they are straight and not on the bias, try using this next step instead of using Bias Press Bars®.

▶ Using the ¾" wide green strips, fold them in half, wrong sides together. Press the fold (Fig. 95).

▶ Place the raw edge of the green strip on the pattern line for the stem. Using a running stitch, sew along the raw edge with a scant ¼" seam allowance (Fig.96a).

▶ Press the folded part of the green strip up and over the sewn portion. This creates a nice rolled stem on one side, with another clean edge for stitching the other side of the stem in place.

▶ Appliqué stitch the folded edge (Fig. 96b) with the appliqué stitch of your choice.

▶ Place the leaves on next, then the large flower, small flower, and the center circle, in that order.

▶ Assemble blocks as shown in Fig. 97 and Fig. 98, page 96, and bind.

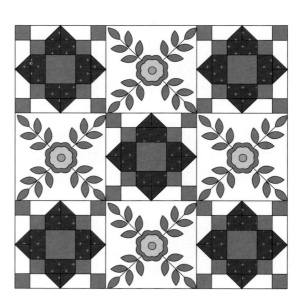

RIGHT: Fig. 97. Assembly diagram for DOWN THE GARDEN PATH, wallhanging size.

BELOW: Fig. 98. Assembly diagram for DOWN THE GARDEN PATH, bed quilt size.

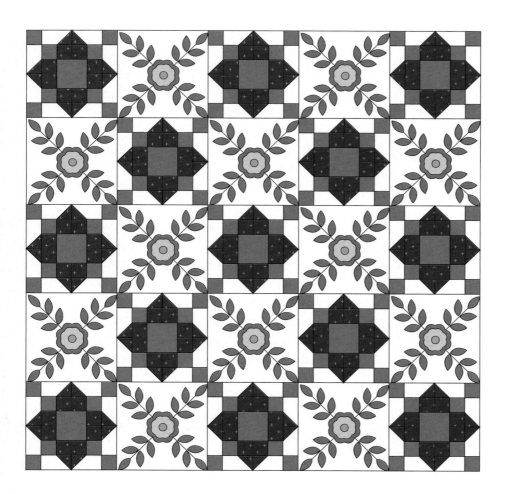

DOWN THE GARDEN PATH appliqué templates
for flowers. Add seam allowances.

Placement diagram for the full layout.

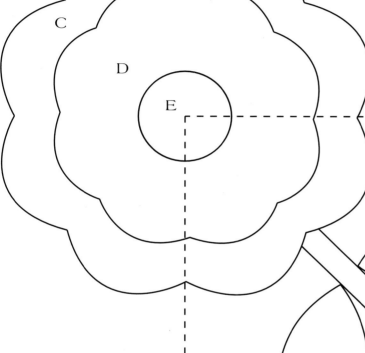

Placement diagram for the appliqué block for
DOWN THE GARDEN PATH. Actual size 12"
block. Repeat four times.

Dimensional Log Cabin

This project came about from a block that my husband designed. The single block pattern appeared in my first book. The effect of using only this block in an entire project was exciting and very interesting. I love the dimension this has over the traditional Log Cabin.

SUPPLIES
- ▶ Sewing machine
- ▶ Fabric markers
- ▶ Cutting board
- ▶ Rotary cutter
- ▶ Ruler
- ▶ Silk pins
- ▶ Fabric scissors
- ▶ Paper scissors
- ▶ Thread to match
- ▶ Template plastic
- ▶ Pencil
- ▶ Pencil sharpener

FABRICS
Select a size for your project and refer to the yardage chart to determine fabric requirements. You need a total of five different fabrics. Choose one light, one dark, and two mediums for the strip section. The fifth center fabric should be a contrasting color to the dark and light fabrics being used in the strips.

Project	Yardage for strips	Center
Wallhanging	⅝ yard each fabric	⅛ yard
Lap Throw	⅞ yard each fabric	¼ yard
Double	1⅝ yards each fabric	¼ yard
Queen	2⅛ yards each fabric	⅜ yard
King	2¾ yards each fabric	⅜ yard

Plate 9. DIMENSIONAL LOG CABIN, 31" x 31". Karen Kay Buckley

CUTTING INSTRUCTIONS

THESE CUTS APPLY *ONLY* TO THE ONE LIGHT, ONE DARK, AND TWO MEDIUM FABRICS, NOT THE CENTER CONTRASTING COLOR FABRIC.

FROM EACH FABRIC CUT THE FOLLOWING:

Wallhanging:

11 strips 1½" wide from each fabric

Lap throw:

16 strips 1½" wide from each fabric

Double:

29 strips 1¾" wide from each fabric

Queen:

39 strips 1¾" wide from each fabric

King:

52 strips 1¾" wide from each fabric

▶ Make a template for the project size of your choice (Large Template A or Small Template B).

▶ Cut the triangles for the center square area.

▶ For the wallhanging and lap throw, cut squares 2¼", and then cut them into quarter-square triangles (Fig. 99).

▶ For the bed sizes, cut squares 2½", and cut them into quarter-square triangles (Fig. 99).

SEWING INSTRUCTIONS

▶ Sew the light, two mediums and one dark fabric together (Fig. 100). (The light and dark fabrics must be on the outside, with the two medium fabrics in the middle.) Press the seams toward the dark fabric.

▶ Use your template and mark the strips (Fig. 101). Place the template up and then down, flipping until you reach the other side of the strip. For the wallhanging and lap throw you should be able to get six sections per strip. For the bed sizes you should get five sections per

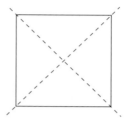

Fig. 99. Cut the center square into quarter-square triangles.

Fig. 100. Assembly diagram for creating dimensional colored strips. Press the seams toward the darker fabrics.

Fig. 101. Using the correct size template, mark five template shapes per strip for wall hangings and lap quilt. Mark six template shapes per strip for king, queen, and double bed quilt.

Fig. 102. Add the contrasting colored triangle separately to the cut strip triangles. Bias edge should be carefully handled to prevent stretching the shape.

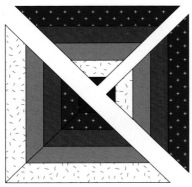

Fig. 103a

Fig. 103b

Fig. 103a and b. Form the Log Cabin block by joining light and dark pieces. Notice the placement of the smaller lights (Fig. 103a) and the larger light sections (Fig. 103b) in this diagram.

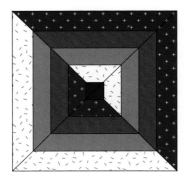

Fig. 104. The Dimensional Log Cabin block fully assembled.

strip. As a result of the odd amount, start every other strip with the template up and then the next strip with the template down. **Construction tip:** if the template appears to be too big for the size of the strips, first check the width of your strips (they may not be cut properly), then check to see if you are sewing more than a ¼" seam allowance.

▶ Add a triangle to each of the previous sections by centering the triangle over the smaller section (Fig. 102). Press the seam toward the triangle.

TO MAKE ONE BLOCK YOU NEED:

▶ Two sections with the lighter section being smaller (Fig. 103a) and two sections with the dark section being smaller (Fig. 103b).

▶ Pin and sew the two sections together with the lighter strip toward the center, and pin and sew the two sections together with the darker strip toward the center forming two larger triangles (Fig. 104). Press the seams of these triangles in opposite directions, to make the last step easier.

▶ Pin and sew these two triangles together and press the long diagonal seam toward the darker center strip side.

▶ Assemble and sew the blocks in rows according to the following diagrams for the project size of your choice.

DIMENSIONAL LOG CABIN, lap throw, 24 blocks.

DIMENSIONAL LOG CABIN, wallhanging, 16 blocks.

DIMENSIONAL LOG CABIN, queen-size bed quilt, 48 blocks.

DIMENSIONAL LOG CABIN, king-size bed quilt, 64 blocks.

DIMENSIONAL LOG CABIN, double-size bed
quilt, 36 blocks.

LEFT: DIMENSIONAL LOG CABIN, wallhanging variation, 16 blocks.

Home Is Where the Heart Is

This wonderful little piece combines machine piecing and appliqué. The appliqué may be completed by hand or machine. This is a great project for a housewarming present or just to hang in your own home.

The finished size of this piece is 31½" x 31½".

SUPPLIES

- ▸ Cutting board
- ▸ Rotary cutter
- ▸ Ruler
- ▸ Sewing machine
- ▸ Thread to match, for piecing and appliqué
- ▸ Paper scissors
- ▸ Pencil
- ▸ Bias Press Bars®
- ▸ Small pieces of freezer paper
- ▸ Supplies for the appliqué method of your choice

FABRICS

⅜ yard for roof, heart, center square of log cabin blocks, and binding

⅛ yard for sky

¼ yard green for leaves

¼ yard for stem

⅛ yard first light

½ yard second light

½ yard third light

¼ yard first dark

⅜ yard second dark

⅜ yard third dark

1 yard for the backing

Plate 10. HOME IS WHERE THE HEART IS, 31½" x 31½". Karen Kay Buckley

LOG CABINS:
HOME IS WHERE THE HEART IS

INSTRUCTIONS

▸ Make a template of the heart (3-0) and leaf (3-1), pattern provided on page 112. Do not add a seam allowance to the template.

▸ Make a template from freezer paper for the house pieces C and D, page 113. Do not add a seam allowance to the template.

CUTTING INSTRUCTIONS

▸ Cut all of the strips 1¼" wide unless otherwise marked.

▸ Cut 1 strip of the center fabric (trim to 27" long)

▸ Cut 2 strips of the first light (trim 1 to 27" long)

▸ Cut 3 strips of the first dark

▸ Cut 4 strips of the second light

▸ Cut 4 strips of the second dark

▸ Cut 5 strips of the third light

▸ Cut 5 strips of the third dark

▸ From the sky fabric, cut the following pieces (Fig. 105):

▸ Cut 3 A pieces – 2½" x 1½" rectangle.

▸ Cut 2 B pieces – cut a 2⅞" square, and then cut it into half-square triangles.

▸ From the roof fabric, cut one C piece. Press the freezer paper template onto the top of the fabric and cut around the shape, adding a ¼" seam allowance when you are cutting (Fig. 106). Note: When using freezer paper, remember that the waxy side sticks to the fabric. The paper side is easier for tracing and writing.

FROM THE MEDIUM BROWN, SECOND DARK, CUT THE FOLLOWING:

▸ Cut 1 D piece, using the freezer paper template you made adding ¼" seam allowance when you cut.

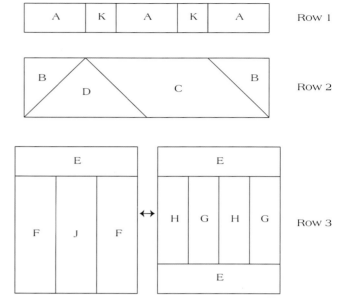

Fig. 105. HOME IS WHERE THE HEART IS assembly diagram for completed house block.

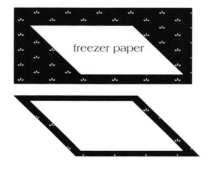

Fig. 106. Iron the freezer paper template to the top of the fabric and then use it as a guide for trimming the ¼" seam allowance.

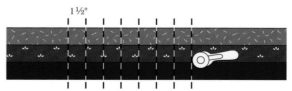

Fig. 107. To make the pieced inner border, first sew three rows together, then cut into 1½" sections.

▶ Cut 1 E piece – 4½" x 1½"

▶ Cut 2 F pieces – 4½" x 1¾"

FROM THE THIRD DARK, CUT THE FOLLOWING:

▶ Cut 2 E pieces – 4½" x 1½"

▶ Cut 2 G pieces – 3½" x 1½"

▶ Cut 2 K pieces – 1½" x 1½"

FROM THE FIRST LIGHT, LIGHTEST LIGHT, CUT THE FOL-
LOWING:

▶ Cut 2 H pieces – 3½" x 1½"

FROM THE SECOND LIGHT, MEDIUM LIGHT, CUT THE
FOLLOWING:

▶ Cut 1 J piece – 2" x 4½"

▶ Cut 4 strips 3" x 26" – this allows a little
extra for the miter. This is for the third
border area, outside the pieced square
border.

FROM THE THIRD LIGHT, DARKEST LIGHT, CUT:

▶ Cut 4 strips 3½" x 16½" – this allows a little extra for the miter. This is for the first
border area.

FROM EACH OF THE THREE DARK FABRICS, CUT THE
FOLLOWING:

▶ Cut one 1½" wide strip, by at least 35", for
the pieced square border.

FOR THE APPLIQUÉ AREA CUT THE FOLLOWING:

▶ Cut 26 leaves. (Trace around the template on the wrong side of your fabric. It
is best to layer your fabric, four thicknesses, and cut four leaves at one time.)
Follow the instructions for the appliqué
technique of your choice. See pages 24 -
31.

▶ Cut several bias strips that are 1¼" wide.
Sew the strips together until they are 60"
long. Use the ³⁄₁₆" Bias Press Bar® for the
stems. Refer to the instructions for making bias press stems, page 31.

▶ Sew the house section together (Fig.
105). Because of the angles of the
shapes, row two can be tricky. To make
it easier, keep the freezer paper template

in place during this phase of the piecing
or mark ¼" sewing lines on the wrong
side of the fabric.

▶ Attach the first border. To control the
seams, sew with the house facing you.
Remember to sew from the ¼" to the ¼"
to ensure good mitered corners. (Refer
to Attaching and Mitering Borders and
Corners, page 43.) This is your appliqué
border area. I recommend you complete
all of the piecing and then return to the
appliqué.

▶ Attach the pieced square border. Sew
three previously cut 1½" x 35" strips
together, from the lightest to the darkest.
Press the seams toward the darker fabric
and cut into 1½" wide sections (Fig. 107).

▶ Sew five sections together to make one
side. Make a total of four sides. (Refer to
Fig. 108, page 110 for placement of the
pieced borders.)

▶ Attach side one. One square will extend
above the previous section. Attach the
second and third pieced borders. When
you attach the fourth pieced border, return
to the beginning and close the seam
between it and the first pieced border.

▶ Attach the next border area. These are
the strips you cut 3" wide. Miter the corners.

TWENTY LOG CABIN BLOCKS ARE NEEDED FOR FINAL
BORDER. BUILD LOG CABIN BLOCKS AS FOLLOWS:

▶ Sew the 27" center square strip (1) and
the first 27" light strip (2) together. Press
all seams for the Log Cabin blocks away
from the center fabric. Cut the strips into
1¼" sections (Fig. 109, page 110).

▶ Sew this section to the first light strip 3.
Place the strip (3) right side up and place
the sections from the previous section
(1-2) face down (Fig. 110a, page 111).

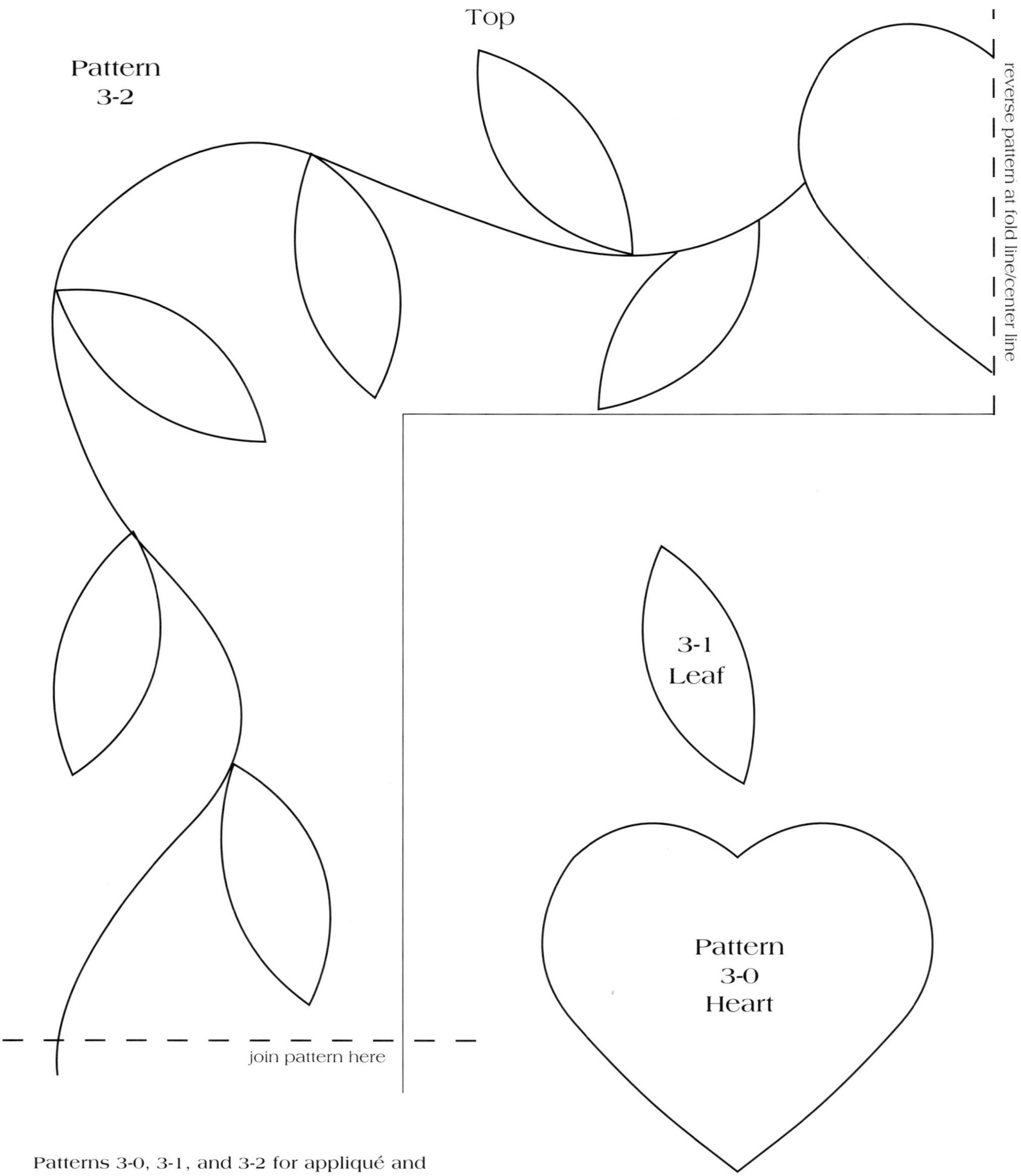

Top

Pattern
3-2

reverse pattern at fold line/center line

3-1
Leaf

Pattern
3-0
Heart

join pattern here

Patterns 3-0, 3-1, and 3-2 for appliqué and placement guide for HOME IS WHERE THE HEART IS quilt.

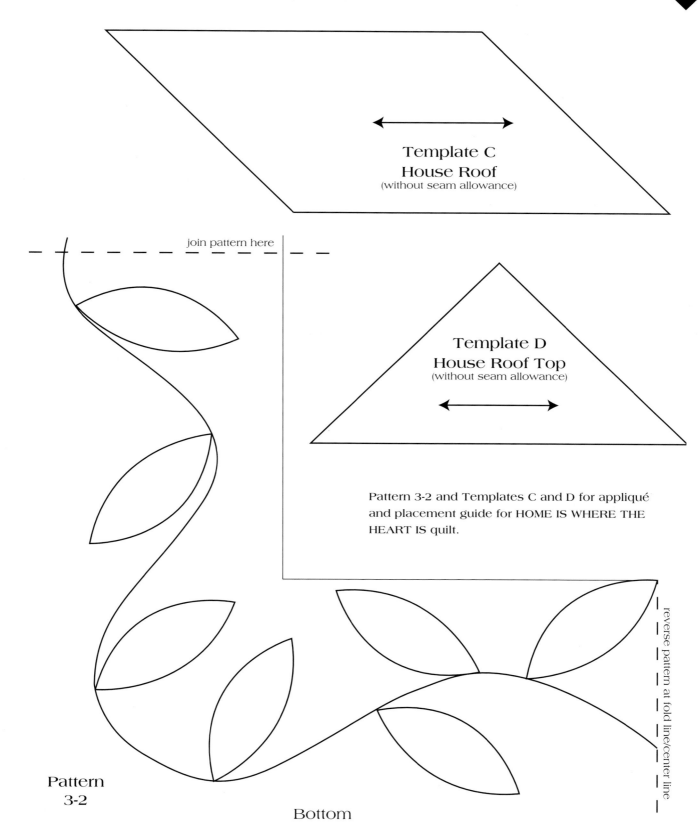

Template C
House Roof
(without seam allowance)

join pattern here

Template D
House Roof Top
(without seam allowance)

Pattern 3-2 and Templates C and D for appliqué and placement guide for HOME IS WHERE THE HEART IS quilt.

reverse pattern at fold line/center line

Pattern
3-2

Bottom

Ladders, Leaves, and Logs

Working from your scraps can make this a fun project. I used scraps from my light and dark purple collection. A student, Mary Rhyner, made hers using blue scraps. Yardage is given in case you do not yet have a scrap collection.

The finished size of this piece is 88" x 88".
Consider altering the outer border if you need your quilt to be larger or smaller.

SUPPLIES

▸ Cutting board
▸ Rotary cutter
▸ Ruler to use with rotary cutter
▸ Sewing machine
▸ Sewing thread for piecing
▸ Items for appliqué method of your choice
▸ Bias Press Bars®
▸ Pins

FABRICS

4 yards for outer border, binding, and inner border strips

1¾ yards for light inner border (appliqué section). You will have extra from this fabric to use as one of your light prints.

½ yard of 10 different light prints (or scraps to total that amount)

½ yard of 10 different dark prints (or scraps to total that amount)

¼ yard for stems

2 different ⅛ yard pieces for leaves

Plate 11. LADDERS, LEAVES, AND LOGS, 88" x 88". Karen Kay Buckley

CUTTING INSTRUCTIONS

FROM EACH ½ YARD FABRIC CUT THE FOLLOWING:

▶ One 2" strip. Cut the strips in half so the two pieces are about 22" long. The reason for cutting these in half is to give a more scrappy effect.

▶ One 3⅞" strip, and then cut the strip into squares and cut the squares in half on the diagonal. You will need 64 light and 64 dark triangles.

▶ Eight strips 1¼" for the Log Cabin border section.

FROM THE LIGHT INNER BORDER FABRIC CUT:

▶ Four strips 6½" wide. The strips will now be 6½" wide x 63" long.

FROM YOUR 4 YARD PIECE OF FABRIC CUT:

▶ Four strips 2" x the width of the fabric. The strips will be 2" x approximately 44" long.

▶ Take one yard of this fabric and put it aside for binding.

▶ For the remaining border areas, fold the fabric so the strips will be approximately 98" long. You need to cut four strips 2" wide and four strips 8½" wide.

Center Portion

▶ Using the 2" x 22" strips, sew one light strip to one dark strip. To give this a scrappy effect, do not sew the same light and dark print together more than one time.

▶ Press the seams toward the darker fabric.

▶ Cut these strips into 2" sections (Fig. 113). You will need 160 of these units.

▶ Sew these units into four-patch units (Fig. 114). Since they are pressed toward the dark, you should not need to pin because the seams will butt together. You will need 80 of these units.

▶ Using the triangles you cut from the 3⅞"

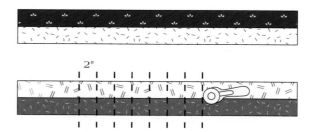

Fig. 113. Cut the sewn strips into 2" sections. Vary the light and dark fabrics for a scrappy look.

Fig. 114. Assemble cut sections into four-patch units. Press seams toward the darker colors.

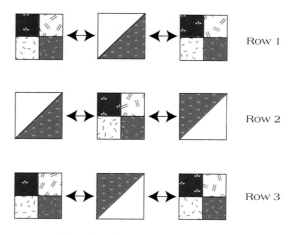

Row 1

Row 2

Row 3

Fig. 115. Follow the placement diagram for each row. The four-patch units connect to the half-triangle units to form the nine-patch block, Jacob's Ladder.

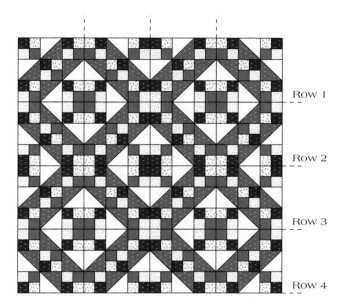

Row 1
Row 2
Row 3
Row 4

Fig. 116. Sixteen blocks connect to form the ladder portion in the center of the quilt. Follow placement diagram carefully, row by row, to assemble it accurately.

2" x 44"
6½" x 98"
2" x 98"

Fig. 117. The area for the appliqué border is formed by sewing together three strips of fabric. Repeat four times. (This unusual shape will be mitered at both ends later.)

strip, sew one light triangle to one dark triangle. Press the seams toward the dark triangle.

▶ Refer to Figure 115 for block construction. Watch your color placement to make sure the light and dark fabrics are in the correct place. (This is the voice of experience. I sewed one four-patch section incorrectly and had to do some ripping after the entire top was assembled. I hate it when that happens.) You will need 16 of these blocks. Placing pins at the points may be helpful to get the points to meet.

▶ Refer to layout (Fig. 116) for placement of the blocks. This will complete the center portion of the quilt.

Appliqué Border Area

▶ Sew one dark strip to each side of a light strip (Fig. 117). One 2" strip will be 44" and one strip will be 98" long. Press the seams toward the dark fabric. Transfer the appliqué design to the border, using Saral® paper or a light box. Refer to Section 1 for details on transferring patterns.

▶ The appliqué pattern pieces indicate how many of each to cut. Remember the slash marks indicate those edges that do not need to be turned under because they will be covered by another appliqué shape. Do not appliqué the J leaves or G tulips in the corner. They will be appliquéd after the borders are mitered.

▶ Attach and miter the inner borders. Add the G (tulip) and J (leaf) pieces to complete the corner areas after sewing and pressing the seams.

Piecing Log Cabin Blocks for the Pieced Border Area

For those of you who have sewn regular Log Cabin blocks before, these are offset Log Cabin blocks so they are a little different.

I made 10 to 12 of these blocks in exactly the same colors. This means the 1¼" strips you cut can be cut from 44" to about 17" long. Because there are 112 of these blocks, the blocks that are identical in color can be separated when sewn into the border. By making them identical it will save a lot of sewing time, but still keep that scrappy effect. The only word of caution is do not use the same light print and the same dark print on the outside of these blocks frequently. It will help when sewing the border design together.

▶ Sew one 1¼" light strip to one 1¼" dark strip (Fig. 118). Press the seams toward the dark strip. Cut these strips into 1¼" sections.

▶ Sew these units onto a dark strip, with the light square from the previous units toward the top.

▶ Cut and press these units. They should now look like Figure 119.

▶ All seams from here on out should be pressed away from the first dark square.

▶ Sew the preceding units to a light strip. The light square will be towards the top.

▶ Cut and block should now look like Figure 120.

▶ Sew these units to a dark strip.

▶ Cut and the units should now look like Figure 121.

▶ Sew these units to a light strip.

▶ Cut and units should now look like Figure 122.

▶ Sew these units to a dark strip.

▶ Units should now look like Figure 123.

▶ Sew these units to a light strip.

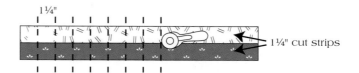

Fig. 118. Sew your favorite light and dark colors together for the center of the offset Log Cabin block. You will need to cut a total of 112 units.

BELOW: Fig. 119–127. These figures show the assembled offset Log Cabin blocks, after cutting the excess fabric. Remember to alternate adding strips of light and dark fabrics.

Fig. 119.

Fig. 120.

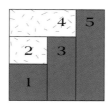

Fig. 121.

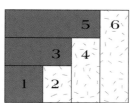

Fig. 122.

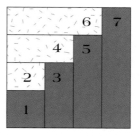

Fig. 123.

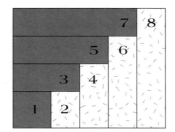
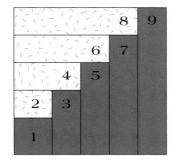
Fig. 124.

- ▸ Cut and the units should now look like Figure 124.
- ▸ Sew these units to a dark strip.
- ▸ Cut and units should now look like Figure 125.
- ▸ Sew these units to a light strip.
- ▸ Cut and units should look like Figure 126.
- ▸ Sew these units to a dark strip.
- ▸ Cut and the blocks should now look like Figure 127.
- ▸ Refer to Figure 128, page 120 for the placement for the offset Log Cabin blocks.
- ▸ Attach the outer border and you are ready to baste and quilt.

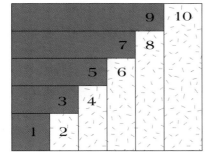
Fig. 125.

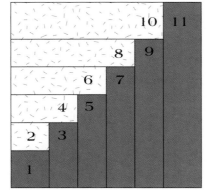
Fig. 126.

Fig. 127. The finished block.

Fig. 128. Placement diagram of the offset Log
Cabin blocks. Attach the outer border strip and
you are ready to baste and quilt.

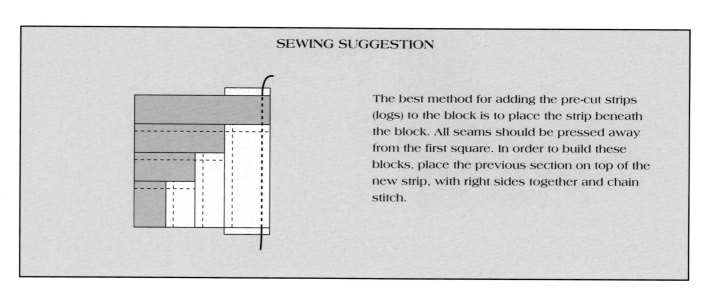

SEWING SUGGESTION

The best method for adding the pre-cut strips
(logs) to the block is to place the strip beneath
the block. All seams should be pressed away
from the first square. In order to build these
blocks, place the previous section on top of the
new strip, with right sides together and chain
stitch.

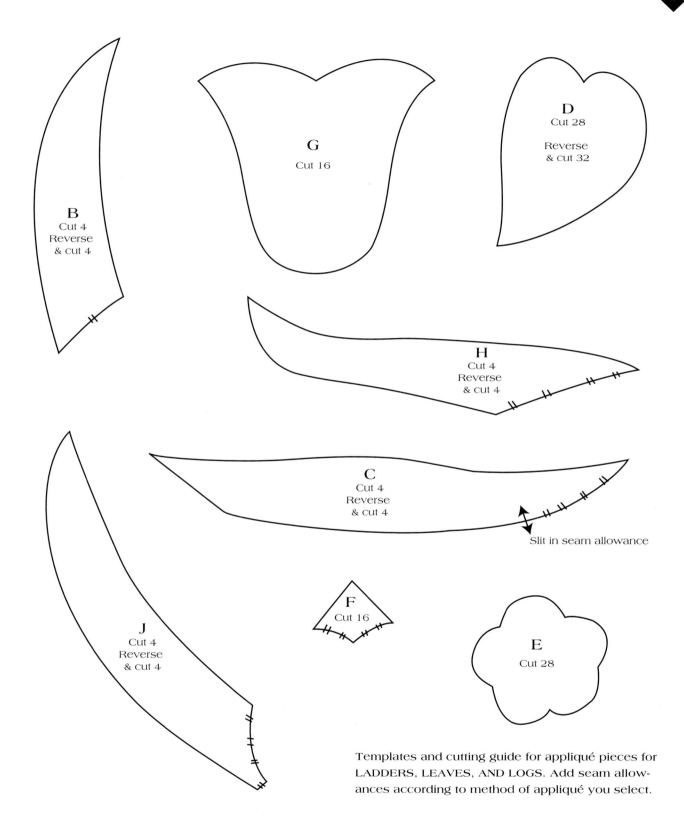

B
Cut 4
Reverse
& cut 4

G
Cut 16

D
Cut 28

Reverse
& cut 32

H
Cut 4
Reverse
& cut 4

C
Cut 4
Reverse
& cut 4

Slit in seam allowance

J
Cut 4
Reverse
& cut 4

F
Cut 16

E
Cut 28

Templates and cutting guide for appliqué pieces for
LADDERS, LEAVES, AND LOGS. Add seam allowances according to method of appliqué you select.

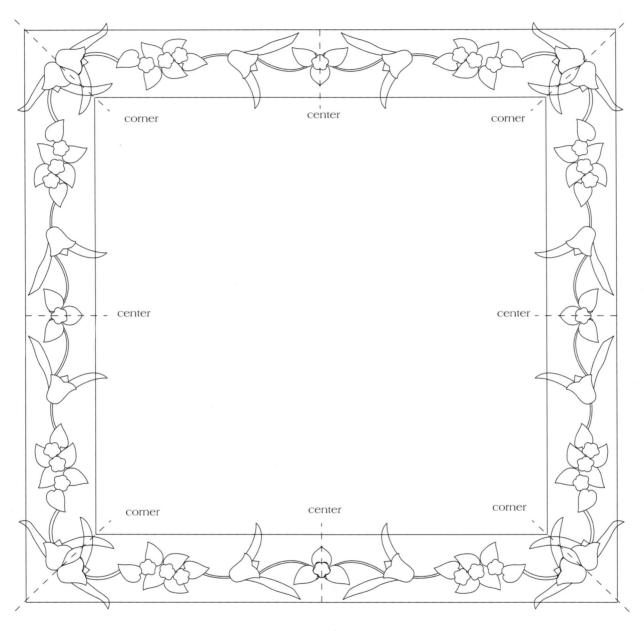

corner   center   corner

center   center

corner   center   corner

Placement diagram for appliqué pieces for LADDERS, LEAVES, AND LOGS. Full size placement guides follow on next three pages, shown without seam allowances. Note: some flowers overlap or repeat on the next section. Also, the corner appliqué design(s) are marked and added after the border pieces are sewn, mitered, and pressed.

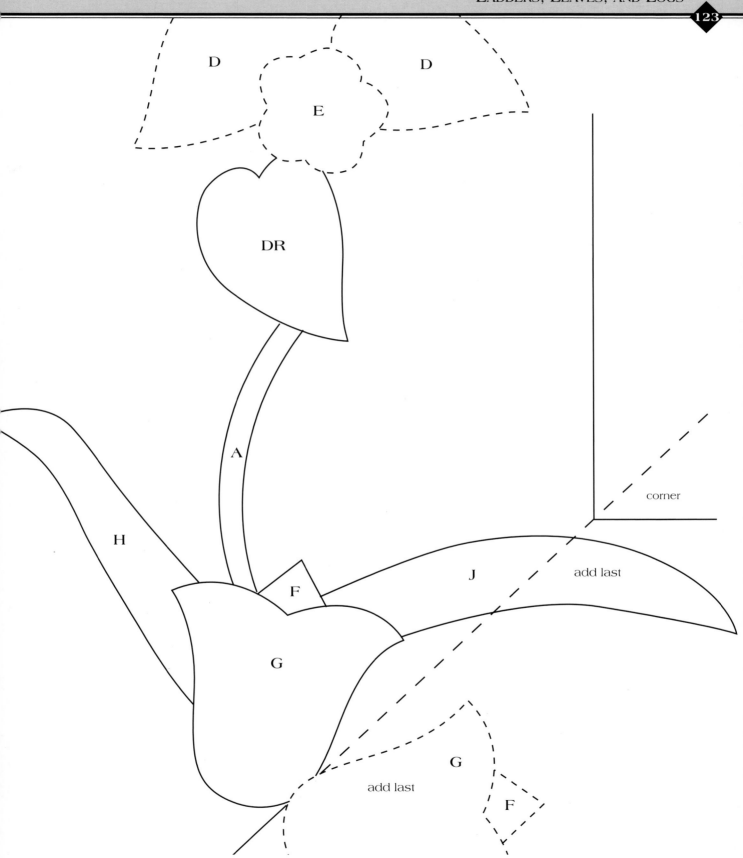

F

B

G

D

E

D

DR

E

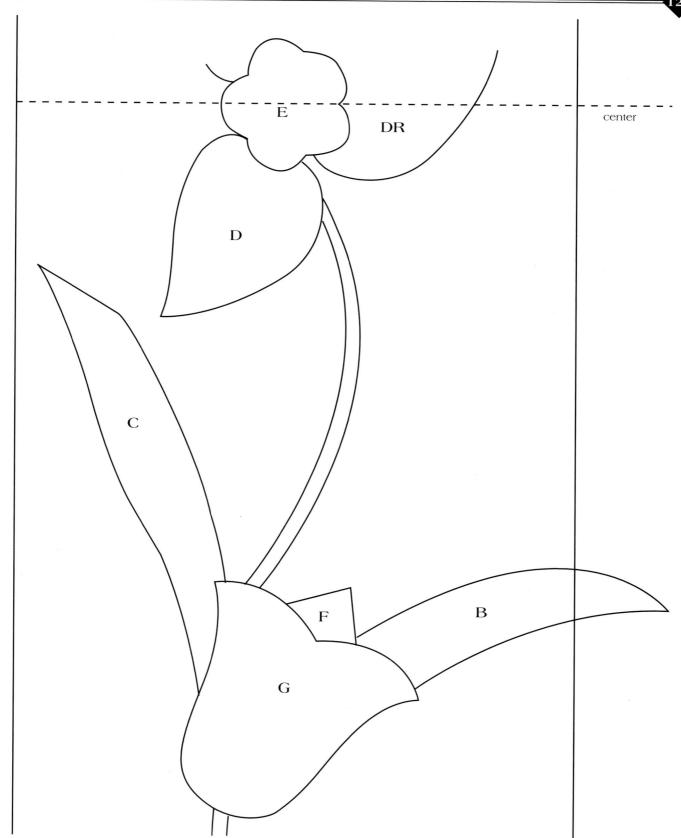

center

Flowering Heart

This beautiful little wallhanging would make a great gift, or be wonderful hanging in your own home. It could be done in pink and burgundy shades to be used as a Valentine's Day wallhanging. It would be a perfect piece on which to learn machine appliqué. Whether it is hand or machine appliquéd, it will look fantastic!

The finished size of this piece is 32" x 32".

SUPPLIES

▸ Supplies for the appliqué technique of your choice
▸ Fabric markers
▸ Fabric scissors
▸ Paper scissors
▸ Cutting board and rotary cutter are optional
▸ Ruler
▸ Sewing machine
▸ Thread to match your appliqué fabric
▸ Silk pins
▸ Glue stick
▸ Bias Press Bars®

FABRICS

1 yard for the background
⅛ yard pieces of two green and seven different colors for the heart area and border
⅜ yard pieces of two greens for the bias border area
¼ yard for binding
1 yard for backing

Plate 12. FLOWERING HEART, 32" x 32". Karen Kay Buckley

INSTRUCTIONS

► Transfer the design to your background fabric.

► Appliqué the pieces in the order they are numbered. Each piece has a letter and number, because there are several pieces of some of the shapes.

► After the center section is completed, you are ready for the border. Make a template for the N, O, and P shapes. Do not add a seam allowance to these templates. Cut four N shapes, twelve O shapes, and eight P shapes. Do not add a seam allowance to the fabric. The raw edges will be covered by the green bias strips. Glue each of the N, O, and P shapes in place. Apply glue to the background fabric and then place the shape on top of the glue. Remember the glue dries quickly, so do one section at a time.

► Make bias strips for the border area. Using the ¼" Bias Press Bar®, cut the strips 1½" wide. These bias strips go over and underlap each other as they go around the border. In the areas where one bias strip goes under the other strip, it will allow you to hide the raw edges.

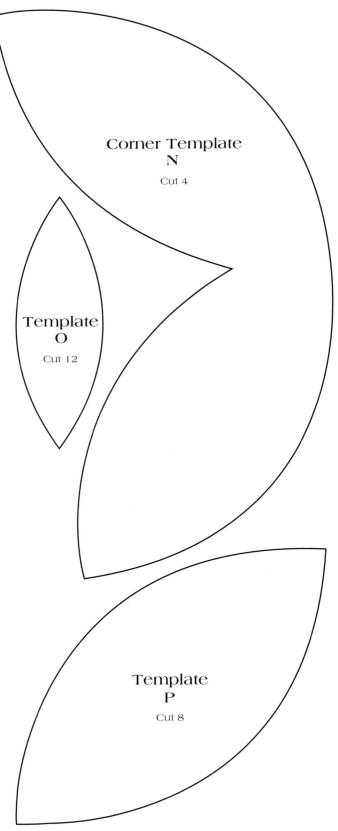

Corner Template
N

Cut 4

Template
O

Cut 12

Template
P

Cut 8

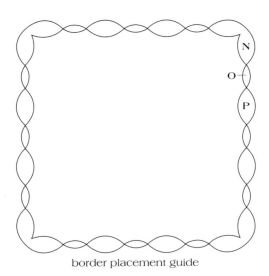

border placement guide

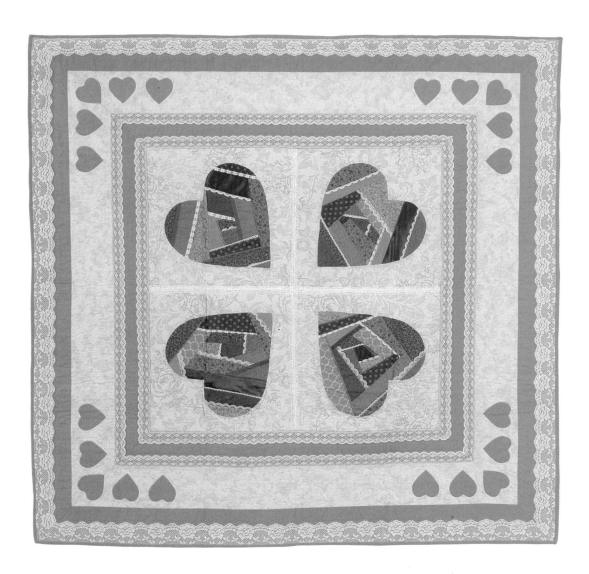

Plate 13. CRAZY LACY HEARTS, 50" x 50". Karen Kay Buckley

INSTRUCTIONS

- ▶ Make a template for heart pattern 4-1. Do not add a seam allowance to the template.
- ▶ Cut the strips for the inner, outer border, and binding. Fold the fabric lengthwise, the same as you always do to cut longer borders.
- ▶ Cut four strips 4½" for the outer border.
- ▶ Cut four strips 4" wide for the inner border. These only need to be 30" long, so use the ends of these strips to cut 20 little hearts (Template 4-0) needed for the light border area.
- ▶ Cut four strips 2" wide for the binding.
- ▶ From the light middle border fabric cut four strips 4½" wide.
- ▶ Cut four squares from muslin and light print, 14½" x 14½". They will be used as foundation bases for the heart blocks.

MARKING INSTRUCTIONS

- ▶ Fold these squares in half on the diagonal. Finger crease the fold. Mark a slash 3½" from the end of the fold. This will be the placement for the bottom of the heart.
- ▶ Trace the heart (Template 4-1, page 139) onto the muslin. The bottom point of the heart should touch the 3½" mark on the diagonal line. You can use a pencil to trace the lines since they will be covered with fabric. It does not matter if they wash out or not (Fig. 129).
- ▶ Crazy patch over the heart shapes. Cut a piece of fabric with straight edges. You can start with a square or rectangle but then cut off one corner, so it will make a more interesting shape as the design builds. (Fig. 130)
- ▶ Place this shape somewhere close to the

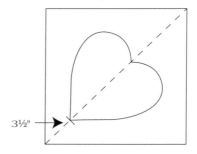

Fig. 129. Mark the foundation fabric for placing the heart design accurately.

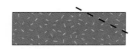

Fig. 130. Cut fabric at angle for interesting shape.

Fig. 131. Only sew from raw edges.

Fig. 132. Top stitch decorative trims in place.

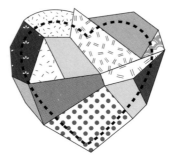

Fig. 133.

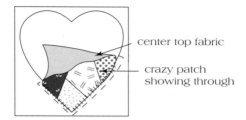

Fig. 134. Reverse appliquéd heart.

Fig. 135. Top-stitch pearl-covered lace in place over the seams.

center

inner border	
middle border	
outer border	

Fig. 136. Finger crease to find the center of each border piece. Match the center creases.

center of the heart outline and pin in place. Select a second fabric in another shade or color. Place the second shape on top of any side except the one you cut off, right sides together. Sew with ¼" seam allowance. You need only to sew from the raw edges of the first shape. Push this second piece of fabric open, away from the first shape. Finger crease the seam. Pin the piece in place so it does not shift during the next steps. Using your ruler, draw a straight line on both sides of the second shape that follow the edges of the first shape; this will be your cutting line. Trim second shape along the sewing line. (Fig. 131)

▶ If you wish to top stitch lace or trims or do a decorative stitch on the seam between the first and second pieces, now is the time. The raw edges of the lace or trim will be caught in the next seams. (Fig. 132)

▶ You are now ready for the third shape. Keep adding the pieces in a circular direction around the first piece until all sides of the first fabric are covered, then fill in any other areas around the outside until the heart shape you traced is covered and the fabrics extend at least ¼" beyond the drawn heart lines (Fig. 133). You are now ready to move to the next step which is reverse appliqué.

Reverse Appliqué

Reverse appliqué means that the lower fabric or fabrics show through an opening in the top piece of fabric. Trace the heart shape onto the top fabric, the same as Fig. 129. Crazy patch the background area and then center the top fabric over the pieced design. Secure the top fabric using four safety pins, one in each corner. Using the lines on the surface of the heart outline, cut ¼" along the *inside* edge of the traced line. Cut approximately 2" sections at a time. Stitch one section and then cut the next 2" section. Continue until the heart has been completely stitched. The center top fabric will fall away, leaving the pieced heart showing through the opening (Fig. 134, page 137).

▸ Cut four 14½" square pieces from the background fabric. Trace the heart shape on the top side of the fabric, using the same 3½" mark that you did when you traced it onto the muslin. Center the background fabric over the crazy patch heart and do reverse appliqué. Remember to cut small sections and sew as you go, turning under the seam allowance as you advance.

▸ Sew the four center hearts together. After they are sewn, top-stitch the lace over the seam. Use embroidery thread to stitch the lace in place.

If you use a pearl-covered lace, like the one in the picture, remove the foot on your sewing machine and free-motion stitch over the pearls. Be very careful if you try this. Because the foot is off the machine, keep your fingers far away from the needle. Stitch two to three stitches on one side of the pearls and then stitch two to three stitches on the other side of the pearls. Keep doing this until the lace covers the seam. If you are not using a pearl lace, keep the foot on your machine and topstitch the lace along the outside edge. (Since the lace with the pearls is stitched down the center area, consider quilting the outside edge to topstitch it now (Fig. 135, page 137).)

▸ Sew the border strips together. Fold the strips in half and finger crease to find the centers of each border strip. Sew one inner, one middle, and one outer border strip together (Fig. 136, page 137).

▸ Sew the border strips to the center heart section. Remember when doing a mitered corner to sew from the ¼" to the ¼", and backstitch at each corner. Do not close the miter yet. The lace is top-stitched to the border before the miter is closed. Sew the lace along one seam. After it is attached, sew the lace to the border beside it, trying to match the corner where the lace meets. Keep going until the lace is all topstitched, and then close the miters.

▸ Make a window template of Template 4-2. Cut the hearts away from the template. Place the window template over the corner of the light middle border and mark the placement of the hearts. Appliqué the previously cut hearts in place.

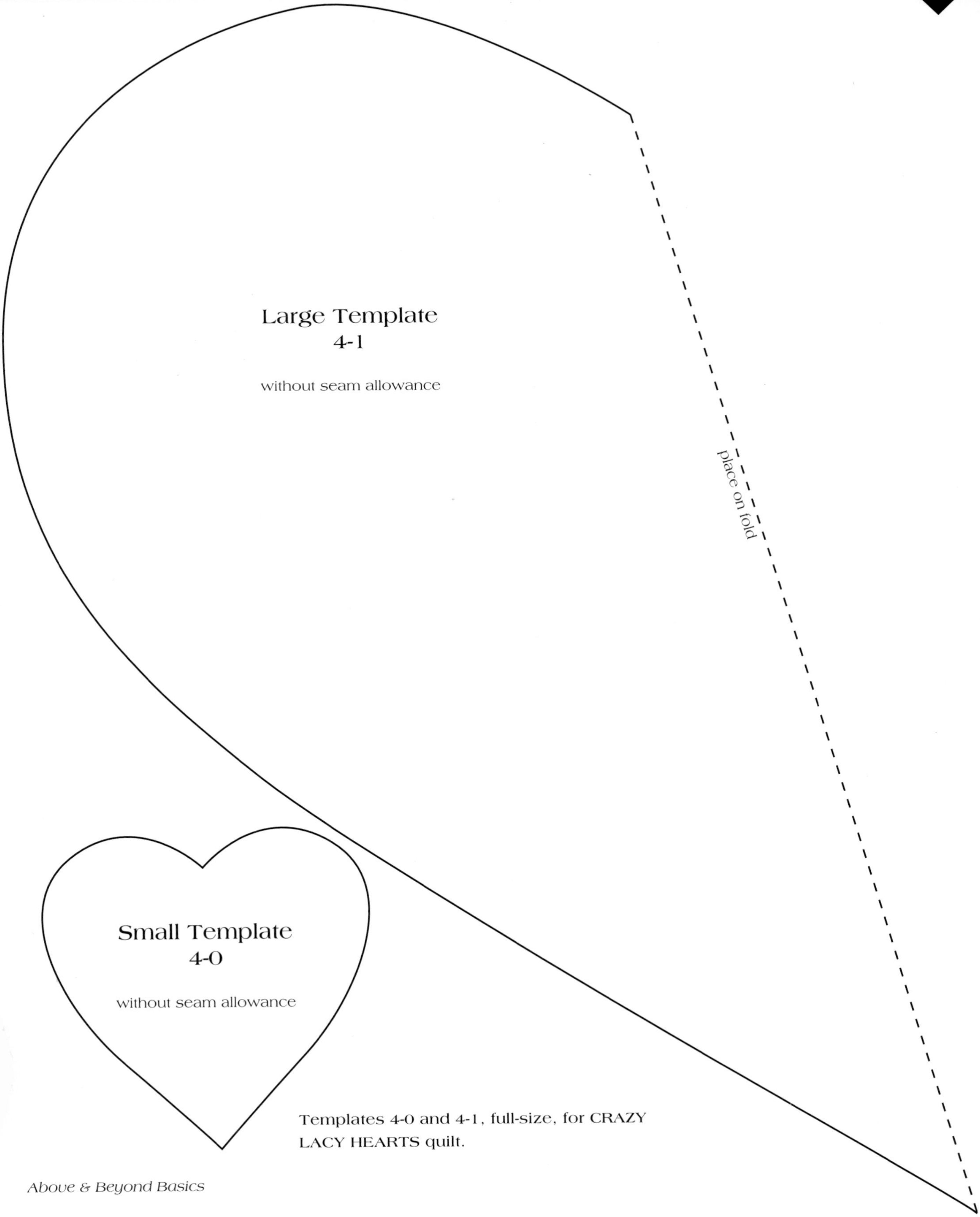

Large Template
4-1

without seam allowance

place on fold

Small Template
4-0

without seam allowance

Templates 4-0 and 4-1, full-size, for CRAZY
LACY HEARTS quilt.

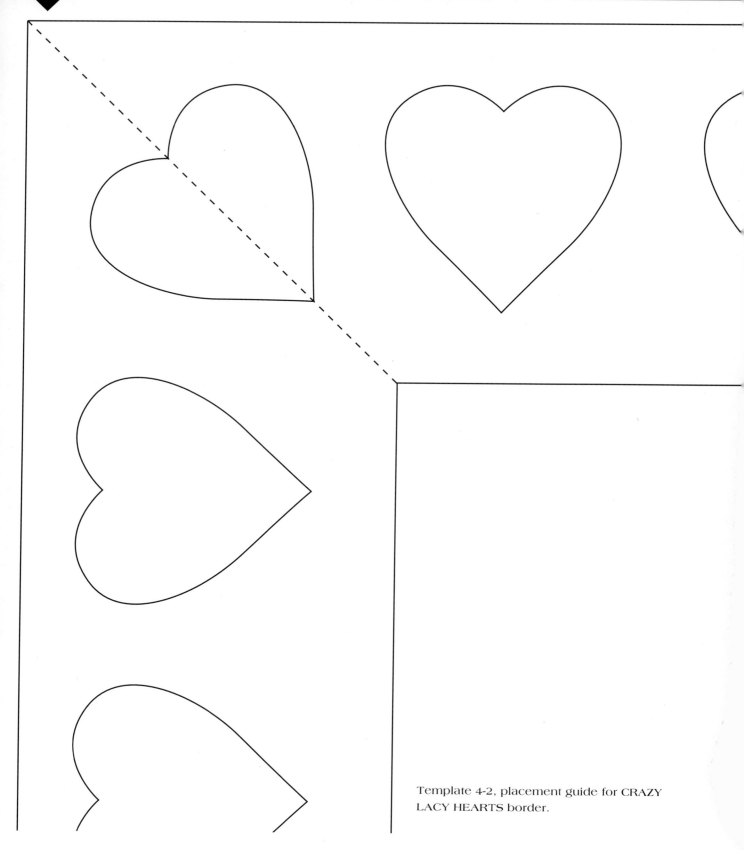

Template 4-2, placement guide for CRAZY
LACY HEARTS border.

HARRISON ROSE, 34" x 34". Michelle Howe

FLOWERING HEART, 32" x 32". Ivy Greenawalt

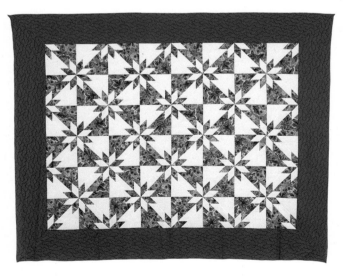

HUNTER'S STAR, 58" x 54". Kathleen Cashman

LADDERS, LEAVES, AND LOGS, 88" x 88".
Mary Rhyner

DOWN THE GARDEN PATH, 80" x 80".
Barbara Schenck

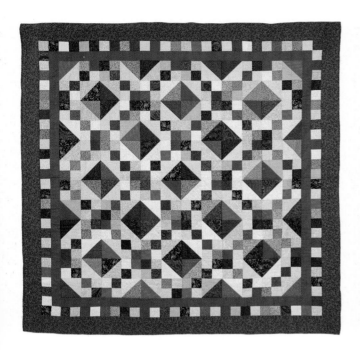

SCRAP HAPPY, 64" x 64". Diane Nesbit

NFL STARS, 75" x 75". Kelly Bailey

DOWN THE GARDEN PATH, 46" x 46". Donna Hemler

HOME IS WHERE THE HEART IS, 31" x 31".
Kay Lynn Orth

AQS Books on Quilts

This is only a partial listing of the books on quilts that are available from the American Quilter's Society. AQS books are known the world over for their timely topics, clear writing, beautiful color photographs, and accurate illustrations and patterns. Most of the following books are available from your local bookseller, quilt shop, or public library. If you are unable to locate certain titles in your area, you may order by mail from the AMERICAN QUILTER'S SOCIETY, P.O. Box 3290, Paducah, KY 42002-3290. Customers with Visa or MasterCard may phone in orders from 7:00–4:00 CST, Monday–Friday, Toll Free 1-800-626-5420. Add $2.00 for postage for the first book ordered and $0.40 for each additional book. Include item number, title, and price when ordering. Allow 14 to 21 days for delivery.